"Lon Allison is a friend and someone who shares his faith both publicly and personally as a way of life. Once we were on an international flight sitting a row apart. While I was witnessing to my seatmate, Lon was sharing his faith just a row behind me. He lives it and teaches it."

—STEVE DOUGLASS, president of Cru

"My friend Lon Allison has written a helpful, practical, and encouraging tool for believers to engage wholeheartedly in evangelism. Through his simple model of praying, caring, and sharing, we learn how to lovingly engage those outside the church with the hope of the gospel. Lon's many years sharing his own faith and teaching others how to effectively and compassionately evangelize make this a must-have resource. (im)POSSIBLE will surely encourage and compel you to embrace the Witness-Life wherever God has called you!"

—ED STETZER, The Billy Graham Distinguished Endowed Chair
for Church, Mission, and Evangelism, Wheaton College

"When starting on an important, exciting, and challenging journey, we all want a guide who has traveled this road before and can show us the way. Lon Allison is our guide, mentor, encourager, and friend on our adventure into introducing more people to Jesus Christ."

—LEITH ANDERSON, president of the National Association of Evangelicals

"Lon Allison lives a life of organic outreach that is an example to me and anyone he encounters. If you have people in your life who need to know that God is real and loves them, this book will prepare your heart, hands, and mouth to be used by God in the work of the Great Commission. Filled with clear instruction and compelling stories, Lon has given us a book that will prepare us to do the one thing we all long for in the depth of our soul: share the life-changing message of Jesus."

—REVEREND DR. KEVIN G. HARNEY, pastor and
author of the "Organic Outreach" trilogy

"The Prayer, Care, Share method h⟨ ⟩ ⟨ ⟩gination of our church. We love Dr. Lon Allison and his commitme⟨ ⟩ f seeing Lon live it out among us! In a world w⟨ ⟩ ⟨ ⟩ır faith, may God use this to turn us around."

⟨ ⟩n Bible Church

"I try to read at least one book on evangelism every year to fire up my own passion for reaching lost people. Lon's book more than accomplished this goal for me! Here are three words to describe it. Comprehensive: this book is the perfect training tool for a course on evangelism—it covers everything! I'm recommending it to my own church's evangelism staff. Personal: Lon lives the Witness-Life he describes in this book. He shares dozens of stories about putting these principles to work. Quite frankly, he's my go-to guy when I'm wrestling with any evangelism issue. Practical: Lon is a great evangelism coach. Prayer, Care, Share may sound like an overworked slogan, but in Lon's hands it becomes a memorable outline for teaching lots of easy-to-apply concepts."

—JAMES L. NICODEM, author of the "Bible Savvy" series and Prayer Coach and senior pastor of Christ Community Church

"Lon loves God and those who are far from God. Both passions merge in (im)POSSIBLE. The principles here ring with authenticity: biblically insightful, relationally respectful, and spiritually meaningful. For those whose struggle with how to best engage others around the hope of Christ, these time-tested insights already used by thousands upon thousands all over the world will both reassure and inspire."

—GARY WALTER, president of Evangelical Covenant Church

"I have been waiting for this book for a long time. I believe Lon and his wife, Marie, personify the message shared in these pages. The Allisons not only believe in the Prayer, Care, Share ministry, they live it. They were leaders in the development of this wonderful, powerful lifestyle that has been adopted by increasing numbers of Christ followers across America and beyond. I encourage you to prayerfully consider the compelling message of this book."

—DR. PAUL CEDAR, chairman of Mission America Coalition

"This is one of the most helpful books on everyday evangelism that I have read. If God is the evangelist, as Lon Allison believes, then our part is to discern how God is at work in the life of others, and then help them to take the next step toward Christ. One of the strengths of this book is the story approach, which shows that evangelism is not just for specially gifted people but for everyday followers of Christ. I warmly commend it to all who want to be part of the 'great connection'—connecting others to fullness of life in Christ."

—LEIGHTON FORD, author and evangelist

I̶m̶possible

Discover the Joy of a Prayer, Care, Share Life

LON ALLISON

NEW HOPE®
PUBLISHERS
Gospel-Centered. Missions-Driven.

BIRMINGHAM, ALABAMA

New Hope® Publishers
PO Box 12065
Birmingham, AL 35202-2065
NewHopePublishers.com
New Hope Publishers is a division of WMU®.

New Hope Publishers serves its authors as they express their views, which may not express the views of the publisher.

Library of Congress Cataloging-in-Publication Data
Names: Allison, Lon (Lon J.), 1952- author.
Title: (im)possible : discover the joy of a prayer, care, share life / by Lon
   Allison.
Other titles: Impossible
Description: First [edition]. | Birmingham, AL : New Hope Publishers, 2016.
Identifiers: LCCN 2016047080 | ISBN 9781625915122 (permabind)
Subjects: LCSH: Witness bearing (Christianity)
Classification: LCC BV4520 .A46 2016 | DDC 248/.5--dc23 LC record available at https://lccn.loc.
gov/2016047080

ISBN-13: 978-1-62591-512-2

N174110 • 0217 • 2M1

Acknowledgments

This is the book I've wanted to write for 20 years. In reality, many people have written it with me. They are the colleagues and mentors who helped forge these ideas and practiced them in their lives. To them I dedicate with thanksgiving to God, *(im)POSSIBLE*.

To my wife, Marie, friend and fellow witness for 38 years. Together we planted a church for the unchurched before we were married. I've watched her bring countless people closer to Christ and often serve as the "spiritual" obstetrician as the births occurred. She exemplifies the Witness-Life.

To my mentor and friend, the late James E. Persson. Jim was my first pastor and was the man who convinced me I was made by God to walk people to Jesus. He apprenticed me in evangelism, church planting, pastoring, marriage, parenting, and walking with Jesus.

To the evangelism associates of the Evangelical Covenant Church. This group of pastors and lay leaders, both women and men, shaped and strengthened many of these principles in scores of churches throughout America. We had a great time together—energizing evangelism in the 1990s!

To my literary mentors in evangelism. They guided me in the early days of my service in evangelism. Many of them I met only in books. People like Joe Aldrich and Jim Peterson, and writers who became colleagues like Bill Hybels, Becky Pippert, Bill Bright, and Kevin Harney.

To the Mead Men—my writing and thinking group composed of men of mighty theological minds, sharp pens, and uproarious laughter—Jerry Root, Walter Hansen, David Henderson, and Rick Richardson.

Finally, to my beloved colleagues and congregation of Wheaton Bible Church. You faithfully love and share Jesus with strangers and friends. Together we are blessed to watch our Lord save hundreds and hundreds of children and adults every year. I am honored and humbled to be a teaching pastor and shepherd of your extensive evangelism and outreach ministries. Let's grow old together.

—LON ALLISON

"In your presence there is fullness of joy." —Psalm 16:11 (ESV)

Table of Contents

PROLOGUE
The Great Adventure

I DIDN'T expect to be shaken by one sentence, but I was. At first I thought the speaker was quoting John 3:16, "For God so loved the world, that he gave his only begotten Son, that whosoever believeth in him should not perish, but have everlasting life" (KJV). Since I'd heard it so often, I gave him light attention. Then he turned the words on their heads, and it was like being awakened by a fire alarm. Instead of quoting John 3:16, he actually said, "God so loved the world, He left us here."

> "GOD SO LOVED THE WORLD THAT HE LEFT US HERE." I AM HERE, AND YOU, IF YOU ARE A SOLD-OUT AND ALL-IN FOLLOWER OF JESUS CHRIST, ARE HERE BECAUSE WE HAVE A PURPOSE WORTH OUR SORROWS AND IMPATIENCE.

He left us here. It must have hit me at a time when I was feeling fragile about this life and world. Terrorist attacks, the loss of my parents and friends to death or incapacity—maybe I was feeling my own sinfulness or mortality that day. All I know was, I didn't want to "stay here." Even Paul said, "We would rather be away from the body and at home with the Lord" (2 Corinthians 5:8 ESV). I have times when I pray for Jesus to come right now. I wonder how much longer He can endure this broken planet filled with decay and depravity. Maybe what I'm really thinking about as I pray is how much longer I can endure the brokenness in both myself and in the world. *Beam me up, Scotty. I'm ready.*

But whatever it was, the speaker's words struck deep. Nearly 20 years later, they still haunt and shake me. "God so loved the world that He left us here." I am here, and you, if you are a sold-out and all-in follower of Jesus Christ, are here because we have a purpose worth our sorrows and impatience. We are here. We are to be witnesses and storytellers of God's rescue mission. That's why we're still here! It's as simple and profound as that. It boggles my mind that God chose us to be the purveyors of His great story to the world. But we have that assignment: "You will be my witnesses in Jerusalem, and in all Judea and Samaria, and to the ends of the earth" (Acts 1:8).

Being a witness of God's story—a story that provides a solution for every sorrow and sin—is a cool but rather *gravitas* sort of assignment. I can get overwhelmed by it. But then I try to remember that God doesn't make mistakes and that He does His best work in us when we admit we can't do it. That weakness opens the portal to power, as His Spirit takes the lead on the witness project.

Scripture is encouraging in this matter. It reveals we're part of a long historical chain of gospel storytellers. Moses started the cavalcade and was followed by the prophets (Acts 26:22). Angels took over the task when Jesus was born (Luke 2:11–13). A few shepherds joined them (Luke 2:17). John the Baptist was really good at it (John 1:7–8, 15). The Samaritan woman (John 4) was one of the best early witnesses. She led a whole village to come and listen to Jesus (vv. 29–30). Mary Magdalene, who first witnessed the resurrected Christ, took up the mantle too (John 20). Peter, John, Paul, all the apostles, Stephen, and Philip spent their lives to witness for Him. In the Book of Acts, a host of others whose names we don't know (Acts 11:19–22) did it too. And they did it very well evidently because the text says, "The Lord's hand was with them, and a great number of people believed and turned to the Lord" (v. 21). I guess God can and does use "well-knowns, little-knowns, and unknowns" like you and me. I like realizing I'm part of a long history of good news witnesses and storytellers.

It is also encouraging to realize God tells His story Himself—the Father and the Son both do it, "I am one who testifies for myself; my other witness is the Father who sent me" (John 8:18). The Spirit does too, "When the Advocate comes, whom I will send to you from the Father—the Spirit of truth who goes out from the Father—he will testify about me" (John 15:26). This witness task is one that the Holy Trinity leads. If God Himself participates, then the importance of the task and the message cannot be overestimated.

I hope you don't feel guilty about your lack of witnessing because, as the saying goes, guilt kills but conviction cures. The conviction we feel for not being more consistent witnesses or Jesus storytellers is actually a backhanded affirmation. The fact that we're troubled means that our own hearts or consciousnesses, in which God dwells, are telling us there is an incongruence. They're telling us something is not quite right and that God in His love has every intention of making it right.

I'm sitting at our dining room table as I type these pages. Just above the table hangs a painting given to me and my wife, Marie, on our 25th anniversary. You can imagine how important it is to us. But I just noticed something. It's a bit crooked. The truth is, almost all Christians are a bit off-kilter or a little crooked when it comes to what I call the Witness-Life. We need straightening. A few of us are too brash. Most of us are too quiet. God wants to get it just right in us. He's placed His desire in us in this matter. The "need" to witness is part of our "born again" DNA, if you will. That's why we feel convicted or a bit off-kilter.

When Peter and John were put in prison for their testimony of Jesus, they were warned by the religious authorities to stop witnessing. The text is clear, "Then they called them in again and commanded them not to speak or teach at all in the name of Jesus" (Acts 4:18). Their response is interesting. "But Peter and John replied, 'Which is right in God's eyes: to listen to you, or to him? You be the judges! As for us, we cannot help speaking about what we have seen and heard'" (vv. 19–20). Did you notice the last phrase, "We cannot help speaking about what we have seen and heard"? They couldn't help it because sharing about their experience with Jesus was now a core part of their being.

Think about the things that are a core part of your being. In the physical realm we can't help but drink and eat—it's a core part of our being. Relationally, I can't help but love my wife, children, and grandchildren—it's a core part of my being. Spiritually, I can't help but talk with God because since I've come to faith in Christ, talking to Him is a core part of my being. In each of these areas, I am convicted when I don't do them, because they are a core part of my being. When convicted or straightened out, I turn back to God, and His presence and power fill me with new energy to live life rightly in each of those areas. For Peter and John, the Witness-Life was a core part of their beings. They couldn't be stopped. I believe God wants this to be the same for us. We were made for it.

Later in his writings, Paul elaborates on this reality.

Evidently some fellow Christians thought Paul was going overboard with the witness thing. They thought he was out of his mind. I've known a few people like Paul. They are 24/7 witnesses. I'm not that way, and you don't necessarily have to be either. You will be a witness according to the personality and calling God has given you. But while Paul is clearly beyond most of us in his dedication and skills, he is just like us internally. He responds to his critics and doesn't argue or disagree. Rather, he agrees with them but tells them why he can't stop sharing his faith in Jesus, "For Christ's love compels us, because we are convinced that one died for all, and therefore all died" (2 Corinthians 5:14). Eugene Peterson, in his translation called *The Message*, says it this way, "Christ's love has moved me to such extremes."

It is love that makes sharing about Jesus a core part of our being. But it is not our love that does it. It is Christ's love in us that moves us to this Witness-Life.

> YOU WILL BE A WITNESS ACCORDING TO THE PERSONALITY AND CALLING GOD HAS GIVEN YOU.

Christ's love moved Him to incarnate and come to earth to show us how to live. Christ's love moved Him to let wicked people hang Him on the Cross—for without His death in our place, our sins could not be forgiven. It was Christ's love that moved Him to rise from the dead and promise to be with us always. His love is in us, and His love is passionate and dedicated to save (Luke 19:10). No wonder we can't help but witness. It is not a "have to" (an obligation) but a *have to* (a burning desire). We simply can't not do this.

However, that doesn't mean we don't become afraid and shy away from this calling. Fear is a constant companion to me when it comes to sharing about Jesus. I've been at it for 46 years, and it is still frightening almost every time I open my mouth. We'll talk more about the fear factor as the book moves on, but suffice it to say, fear is a real and present danger and can lead us to keep our mouths shut. But, think of it this way—lots of good things are scary.

I was in the first or second grade when I learned good things could be scary. My class was going to sing and dance on stage in front of all our parents and teachers. The song was "On the Good Ship Lollipop," made famous by Shirley Temple. We had to dress like sailors, all in white, and we wore silly paper sailor caps. We learned the song and even added dance steps and swayed side to side while singing. I was so embarrassed and frightened. My parents made it worse. They took me to a store and bought me an actual sailor's hat for the performance. I would stand out even more with that hat.

The night finally came, and I marched up onto the platform with all my classmates. The piano started the song, and we started singing and swaying. I was petrified—for about half a minute. Then I remember thinking, *Hey, I like this*. I really liked it. I was no longer afraid. I sang louder and swayed more enthusiastically. When the song was done, I was ready to do another and another and another. I remember hearing other parents tell my parents that I was really good at singing and swaying. I was made for it! I don't sing and dance too much anymore, but when I'm in front of a crowd of people starting a sermon or teaching, I still get a bit scared—every time. But once I start to talk, preach, teach, or sing, joy and energy floods me. The fear dissipates.

Telling others about Jesus is kind of the same. It is always scary until you start. We'll discuss the difficulty of starting, and

I'll provide some helps. But it's been my experience after practicing the Witness-Life for 46 years that once we start, nine times out of ten, it is fun and always meaningful. Sometimes it's only a word, or a few words, we share. Sometimes it turns into a discussion with give and take, agreement and disagreement. Other times, a listener may truly be curious and want to know more. Then there are the times the person we are engaging with is so ready to trust Jesus we couldn't stop them if we tried. Whether it's a few words or a long discussion it is always, as my wife says, "scary-fun."

I'm glad you are willing to join me in this *impossible* witnessing adventure. We really are made for it. We join in the long history of believers and angels in telling the story of our Lord as He speaks to and through us. And even as He witnesses independent of us. In fact, the Bible says even donkeys (a.k.a. Balaam's; see Numbers 22) and rocks and stones (Luke 19:38–40) carry God's message. It is scary fun and more, meaningful beyond description to join this assembly. Let's get going.

We need two operating definitions of the Witness-Life. The first has to do with *what* it is, and the second with the *how* to do it.

WHAT IS THE WITNESS-LIFE?
To witness is to cooperate with God and others to lovingly bring people, one step at a time, closer to Jesus Christ.

HOW DO WE WITNESS?
Prayer, Care, and Share-Share-Share

These two definitions will guide us throughout the book. Living the Witness-Life is an adventure. It is enjoyable, scary-fun, and eternally important. Join me now as we look more deeply into the most important of life's activities and get all the training we need for a wonderful adventure. We were made for it and, most of all, it's *(im)POSSIBLE!*

INTRODUCTION

WHAT am I talking about when I call believers to witness or share their faith? You'll see that I often use the term *Witness-Life* as a descriptor of this effort. I use the word *witness* because Jesus gave us this title in Acts 1:8, "You will be my witnesses." The term is used more than 40 times in the New Testament—I know because I've counted them! We need a biblically-based, clear definition of what the Witness-Life includes.

Probably, most of you reading this book see the Witness-Life as talking to others about your belief in Jesus. That's a good starting point, but we dare not stop there. The Witness-Life merits a deeper understanding because it is much more than simply sharing about Jesus and who He is. And, if we're not careful, our conventional definitions of what Witness-Life is can subtly heap guilt on our shoulders and feel more like a checklist than a way of living. Am I saying that we make too little and too much of it? Exactly. Some of the big questions are:

1. Is Witness-Life only talking or does it include more than talking?

2. How much should I share when I witness?

3. How do I know when I've said enough?

4. What if the listener doesn't want to talk or doesn't respond? Does that mean I've failed?

We'll address all these questions and more.

I've had numerous Christians thank me for being, in their words, an evangelist. They usually then add something like, "because I'm just not good at it and would rather leave it to guys like you." That is an example of making too little of it. Why? Because if you leave it to the few, the professionals, we won't scratch the surface of need. The task of reaching the 7 billion-plus people of the world is too large to leave to a few.

Conversely, in recent days two pastors told me they now experience freedom as they understand the definition I'm about to give you. One of them comes from a church tradition in which every Sunday the gospel was offered and converting people were called forward. In his tradition, or his interpretation of it, you weren't truly witnessing unless you "prayed the prayer of salvation" with a person. The other pastor said he started his Christian ministry with an organization that asked for weekly reports on how many people he'd shared with and what was accomplished in each encounter. In my opinion, both of these examples are making too much of it. I understand the heavy burden these assumptions must level on a believer. If you feel you must share your faith all the time, every day, or even every week, and if sharing your faith means you have to drop the whole plan of God's rescue on individuals you encounter, it becomes oppressive. My two pastor friends labored under this kind of weight for a long time.

For years my mentor and pastor told me I had the gift of evangelism. "No way," I always said. Why? Because I had seen the titans of evangelism do their Witness-Life, and I was not in their league at all. One of them was Billy Graham. I went to a

Graham Crusade in Oakland, California, only a couple of years after coming to faith. I still remember where I sat in the upper deck of the coliseum. I was amazed at the response. I had never envisioned that one man could preach a message, give a clear invitation, and then see hundreds respond. They just kept walking past my aisle toward the stadium grass, hundreds and hundreds of them.

Years later I would work with Mr. Graham and his organization, attending numerous crusades and festivals. The large response to his call was always the same. Well, that was not me! When I gave an invitation, a few and occasionally many would respond, but you could count them on your hands. I was not therefore an effective witness by Billy Graham standards.

The other model I had was of Dr. Bill Bright of Campus Crusade for Christ, now called "Cru" in the United States. Bill was a real hero to me. He was known for sharing Jesus all the time with everyone he met. One of his associates told me that when Bill Bright was younger and had to fly all over the world, he would ask for a middle seat in the airplane. Why? Because that gave him two opportunities to share Jesus. Well I was not Billy Graham, and I was not Bill Bright. *Huh*, I didn't even have Bill in my name. Therefore, I was not an effective witness—or didn't think I was.

HE PROVIDES THE "WHO" TO TALK TO, THE "WHEN" TO TALK, AND THE "WHAT" TO SAY.

Still, my mentor was a man to be trusted. I asked him more about Witness-Life and why he thought I was made for it. He helped me study the issue and walked with me as I came to understand I could tell people about Jesus my way, using only my own personality and staying close to God so He'd guide me. He provides the "who" to talk to, the "when" to talk, and the "what" to say. I also learned that the gift of the evangelist mentioned in Ephesians 4 has more to do with equipping and training than it does with being the superstar who always evangelizes and always sees large results. That's part of the reason I'm writing this book.

The book is separated in two sections that help answer the "what" and "how" questions. Chapters 1–3 define the Witness-Life while chapters 4–11 cover how to witness. In the appendix, I've included additional information on hard-to-answer questions and a Scripture devotional guide for the Prayer, Care, Share method.

I encourage you to turn to the devotional guide, which my wife Marie created, in the appendix, and reflect on the passages there in your time with God. It is designed to take no more than 20 minutes per day and will give you five weeks of Scripture to prayerfully consider. It's a wonderful preparation for the book's themes and content. Use it to reflect deeply on God's Word regarding the issues, and it will nourish your soul and strengthen your resolve to adopt and enjoy the Witness-Life.

We also have an abbreviated Prayer, Care, Share training online at wheatonbible.org/resources/prayer-care-share that includes six short videos I did for our church family. While not as comprehensive as the book, they still have value and can be used in conjunction with the book. Each video is roughly ten minutes in length.

WHAT IS THE WITNESS-LIFE?

I started working on this definition more than 20 years ago. A group of pastors and I began crafting a definition we hoped would free every one of God's people to believe and enjoy sharing their faith as a way of life. I'm in debt to those brothers and sisters and to my dear wife, Marie, who is far better at living a Witness-Life than I am. We forged these principles out of the fires of trying and failing, reading and praying, and always learning. We still are! It is my deepest desire and fervent prayer that this definition and how I unpack it leads you toward a fulfilling Witness-Life. You can do this. Here it is again:

> *The Witness-Life: cooperating with God and others to lovingly bring people, one step at a time, closer to Christ*

Let's open up the definition and grasp its freeing reality. There are three key principles in the definition that I'll describe in the next three chapters. Now I know many of you may be saying, "Come on, Lon, just tell me how to do this." I understand those who just want a how-to formula, but that would make too little of it. Grasping this definition in its rich theological context is what will sustain us in our Witness-Life now and more and more as our lives go forward. Even better, with a deep theological foundation, we can be successful and sense the Father's wonderful affirmation, "Well done, good and faithful servant" (Matthew 25:23).

CHAPTER 1

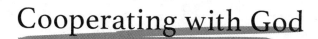

Cooperating with God

NOTICE that the first thing we learn from the definition of the Witness-Life is that God is the "key" and "first" witness to every person. He is always "on the move." He is already there working in the person's life before we get involved, and He sustains and nourishes our witness with His presence once we are placed in the situation.

This morning as I read my devotion, which came from Luke 19, I was reminded that before Zacchaeus climbed up the tree to try and see Jesus, Jesus had come to Jericho seeking Zacchaeus. Jesus stopped under the tree and spoke to Zacchaeus and called him to come down. God initiated this call. He is the original seeker.

In the early church Barnabas and Paul were aware of this seeking presence of God preceding their witness of Him.

> We have come to bring you the Good News that you should turn from these worthless things and turn to the living God, who made heaven and earth, the sea, and everything in them. In the past he permitted all the nations to go their own ways, but he never left them without evidence of himself and his goodness. For instance, he sends you rain and good crops and gives you food and joyful hearts.
> —Acts 14:15–17 NLT

They are saying that the good things of life and the joy they bring us are an evidence of God. Later, as Paul wrote the Book of Romans, he suggested that the witness of God is so evident from the things He has made that people have no excuse to deny God's existence (Romans 1:20). God's witness is everywhere. It is in the beauty of a sunrise and a gentle snow. It is in the birth of a child and the laughter of children at play. It is in the warmth of friendship and family. I've had people who doubted the existence of God ask me if there is a God, then why is everything so hard in life? It's a fair question. It seems at times there is a lot more sad than glad in life. But I turn the thought around a bit. I suggest that in a world of such sorrows, I'm amazed that so much is good and beautiful. If a person pauses and reflects, one can see God everywhere. God is on the move displaying His glory, His attributes, to the world all the time. It is part of His witness to a weary world.

What does this mean for Christian people who want to be effective witnesses of Jesus? It means that people are often more ready for spiritual conversation than we think they are. Why? Because God is already at work in people's lives revealing Himself and His attributes before we come on the scene. We tend to believe that people, especially in the Western world, have little interest in spiritual things. Many well-meaning Christian books go into elaborate detail on the impact of secularism and the various other "-isms" (often one or more of these terms is used— *relativism, pluralism, liberalism, individualism,* and the dreaded *postmodernism*). However defined and however many there are, all of these words communicate that it is terribly difficult and seemingly unlikely to ever reach a friend or relative or neighbor with God's good story, the gospel. I know this is not the intention of such speakers and authors, but often this is the message communicated. Any optimism and hope we had gets kicked right out of us, and the dreaded cultural "-isms" come flying at us. It can lead to discouragement.

But the "-isms" are not really people. They are philosophical constructs and generalizations about worldview. Some knowledge of these constructs can be helpful, but let's remember we are talking with real people, and there is a lot more to a person than a philosophical construct. Every person is precious to God, and every person has thoughts and feelings and experiences that make him or her unique. They are just like us, and we are just like them. The gospel of God is for people not philosophies. Trust that truth, and it will take you a long way toward a meaningful Witness-Life.

People are looking for God because God is looking for people and is revealing Himself (witnessing) to them! Remember that Jesus said the harvest is ready (Matthew 9:37). There is nothing wrong with the harvest. In fact, according to Jesus, it is "ripe" (John 4:35). A farmer friend told me

THE GOSPEL OF GOD IS FOR PEOPLE NOT PHILOSOPHIES.

that when a wheat field is ripe, it is critical for it to be harvested within a certain time frame, or it will spoil. This is the sense of the passages above. These Scriptures ring true in our day as well. People are more ready than we think they are. People are often more ready to hear than we are to share! We can get rid of reticence. In fact, life takes on richer meaning for us when we enter into the lives of people God is already reaching and drawing to Himself.

My wife, Marie, and I have found this to be true time and again. Just when we think a friend, relative, acquaintance, neighbor, or stranger has no spiritual interest, something happens to wake us to a new perspective. In reality, they do have spiritual interest! Recently, we invited neighbors to our home to view a wonderful DVD of the stories of three people with deep needs who discover a relationship with Jesus Christ. The stories display God's ability to bring people out of darkness into His marvelous light. To tell you the truth, we were scared to host the party. Remember, fear almost always precedes witness. Fear is a feeling nearly every Christian faces whenever they are in a witness situation.

We've been in our present neighborhood for ten years. We've hosted dinners and Christmas parties. We pray for our neighbors regularly. We have had many introductory spiritual conversations, but all in all, we've been disappointed. Or at least we were disappointed until the meeting with the DVD. About half the people we invited came. At the end of the DVD, Marie and I shared our stories of how God has remade our lives through Jesus Christ. I then closed the evening by offering ongoing discussion groups if any were interested. We were stunned to see the response. To be brief, the interest led us to start a ladies' and a men's discussion group, which meet regularly in our home or one of theirs. About half of those who came to the initial meeting came to the ongoing discussion groups. Why were we stunned? Because we've read too many books by Christians telling us how hard it is to reach people, and we've had lots of disappointments—but not this time. Heaven is breaking loose in our neighborhood!

One neighbor in particular stands out because neither of us had noticed him previously exhibit any spiritual interest. First of all, he is a 50-year-old scientist, and I don't generally think of scientists as spiritual seekers. Second, he had come to only one of the ten or more parties we'd hosted. Third, I had never talked with him personally for more than five minutes. Fourth, his mother had urged him to attend. I think he came partly as a favor to her. Fifth, he came late to the initial meeting when the 30-minute DVD was half done. I would categorize such a person as least likely to be seeking God and least likely to be found by God.

You know where this is going. He is the one who came up to me at the end and said something like, "If you are serious about having a discussion group, I'm interested. I need something in my life that's different from what I have now." We were blown away. This man was, in our minds, the least likely to respond. We were wrong. He became a regular attender at the discussion group and asked some of the most meaningful and challenging questions you can imagine. I also really like this guy. He is one of my favorite neighbors.

I have to admit that there are still disappointments. This fall, I didn't reconstitute the group of men because of my disappointment with how slow some of the guys were in coming to faith. But just a couple of weeks ago, our scientist neighbor slowed his car as I was installing outdoor Christmas lights. He rolled down his window and among other things said he missed the group and wants it to start again. He wants to keep talking about spiritual matters and, in fact, invites others to come! Why? Because contrary to our wrong thinking and my discouragement, God was and is at work in his life. God is on the move. The Lord is opening his mind at a perfect God-pace, and my neighbor's heart is awakening to needs that 50 years of life have not met. He is now honestly seeking spiritual answers.

My wife and I are privileged to be on the journey with these neighbors and, for me, especially privileged to journey with this man. More, we are energized in our own faith to be in the story of these precious people. At every point, God is on the move. He is a seeking God. Jesus said, "The Son of Man came to seek and to save the lost" (Luke 19:10).

PRINCIPLES FOR COOPERATING WITH GOD

1 Before God brings you into a person's life, He is already there as First Witness.

2 He is proactive, even assertive, in His witness. Jesus said, "The Son of Man came to seek and to save the lost" (Luke 19:10). This is our Lord's mission statement. He was so serious about it that He came to earth Himself to launch the ongoing saving actions of the triune God. He would incarnate and take on a human existence. He would teach the truth about God. He would bleed and die to reach us. Yes, He is the original and never-ending seeker. There is nothing passive about God's seeking. He initiates the saving action because He desires all to be saved and come to the knowledge of the truth (1 Timothy 2:4). Never forget that.

3 His seeking includes an "attracting power" that is at work in the people He seeks. Jesus describes it as a "drawing or dragging" action in a person's life. He said, "No one can come to me unless the Father who sent me draws them" (John 6:44). As I reflect on this reality, I am even more amazed at the love of God. As He moves toward people, He moves the people toward

Him and yet not in such a way as to force people toward Himself—it is a gentle drawing. We evidence this gentle drawing all the time in our church.

Recently a man came to our lobby during the week and asked to see a pastor. Fortunately, Kyle, one of our young pastors, was there and came down to meet with the man, who was a stranger to our church. In their conversation, the man said that he had two choices as he drove up North Avenue. He could turn to the left and go to the bar he too often frequented. His other choice was to turn right, toward our church. He didn't really know what made him turn right, but a sense of absolute necessity seemed to call him to do so. Needless to say, we are glad he did. He has now made a decision to follow Christ. He is at the church almost every day attending whatever is available to help him grow. But the key point is that one day, he felt the urge to turn right. This is the attracting power of God, who is at work. Last Sunday I saw this man sitting in the front row of the church with a Bible in his hand and his eyes intent on worshipping and learning more about the God who loved him and who he now loves.

 God sets divine appointments to include us in the pursuit of those He is reaching. I remember finding a passage in Scripture that opened my eyes to this truth. In 1 Corinthians 3:1–7, Paul is addressing a problem in the Corinthian church. Evidently some of the Christians were making heroes out of those who helped them follow Christ. Factions were forming around the heroes. Some followed a wonderful preacher named Apollos. Others followed Paul. Paul chastised them for thinking from a human point of view rather than a God point of view, he gives them the theological truth found in verse 5, "What, after all, is Apollos? And what is Paul? Only servants, through whom you came to believe—as the Lord has assigned to each his task." Read the last phrase again, "as the Lord has assigned to each his task." We all have our assignments, each of us.

I still remember the Saturday evening many years ago when I was in O'Hare airport in Chicago heading to the East Coast to preach. O'Hare is one of the world's busiest airports. Nearly a quarter of a million passengers fly out of it daily. I wandered toward my gate, found a seat in the waiting area, and pulled out my Bible. I was probably reviewing my text for the next morning. A few seats away from me, I could hear a young woman sharing her faith in Jesus with a man she knew. I believe they were traveling together. I couldn't help overhear because in her enthusiasm to share, she was pretty loud. I began to pick up that he'd been asking her some tough questions she didn't know how to answer. Then, at one point she stood up and looked down the row. Seeing me with an open Bible, she immediately blurted out, "Are you a Christian?" I nodded yes, then she waved me to join them in an almost pleading sort of way saying something like, "Maybe you can help me answer his questions." I did. I don't remember the questions. I don't remember their faces, but I will never forget sitting in that seat on that night in that airport, discovering I'd entered a divinely ordered appointment to help a young believer share her faith.

God has appointments for all of us. God so loves the world that He's left us here. A meaningful life occurs when we start recognizing the appointments and by faith enter into Witness-Life.

 He is always with us in the appointments. I mean, honestly, do you think God would leave us alone when we witness? Eternal salvation is far too important to be left to us. I am always encouraged when I remember the instruction of our Lord in the Great Commission (Matthew 28:18–20). In the passage He tells us, among other things, to "go and make disciples of all nations." It is a daunting commission. Whether one thinks of nations as nation-states like we do today or as ethnic groups, it is an overwhelming task. But He promises to join us in the commission. Remember the last phrase? It is precious to believers. "And surely I am with you always, to the very end of the age." Perhaps you've had the experience of sharing your faith with a friend or stranger and later, after the encounter, have little recollection of what you said? That's because you weren't saying it. God was with you, speaking through you. Or, you may remember times when you said some things you later learned were wrong. I have misquoted verses or said, "Paul said," when it was really Jesus who said it more than I want to remember. Of course, we all have. But our God is so great He can convert even the wrong things we say and things we don't say at all and use them in a listener's mind. God is with us in witness. He's in charge!

 He is responsible for the results—we don't save anybody. Only God can do that. Let's look at John 6:44 again, but this time focus on the first part of the text. Jesus says, "No one *can* come to me *unless* the Father who sent me draws them" (author's emphasis). No one can come without God doing it. Jesus emphasizes this truth two additional times in the same passage. "All those the Father gives me *will* come to me" (John 6:37, author's emphasis). It doesn't say all those the Father gives me "might" come or "may choose" to come. It says "will come." The point is emphatically made in verse 65. "He went on to say, 'This is why I told you that no one can come to me unless the Father has *enabled* them'" (author's emphasis). Thus, three times in John 6, Jesus emphasizes the mystery of God engineering and completing the saving act of regenerating a soul. For more on this, also look at Acts 13:48.

I find it immensely helpful to remember that God does the saving. This takes a lot of the pressure off us from thinking we have to do and say everything right. I think of it as a "benevolent compelling" that I am glad to entrust solely to our God of Grace.

God is the witness. God is the evangelist. We are invited to join Him in His saving actions. When we do, He is right there with us, and He is responsible for the results.

GOD IS THE WITNESS. GOD IS THE EVANGELIST. WE ARE INVITED TO JOIN HIM IN HIS SAVING ACTIONS. So, we can relax and be assured in our Witness-Life. In fact, we can enjoy and find great meaning in it. You and I will be tempted to think this is something we do for God and apart from God. But that is categorically false. This is God's business, and God takes the lead. He has gone ahead of us, and He is the one who orchestrates people to seek Him. Such freedom and hope rises in us when we realize this great truth. Get in on this! Join Him. You were made for it!

CHAPTER 2

And Others
(It Takes a Village to Save a Soul)

THE second big idea for living a joyous Witness-Life is to realize God usually uses several Christians to bring one person to Himself.

The Scriptures reference this reality in two sections about "witness" through the analogy of agriculture. In 1 Corinthians, Paul writes these words:

> *I planted, Apollos watered, but God gave the growth.*
> —1 Corinthians 3:6 ESV

It seems the young and immature believers in Corinth were forming alliances around the leaders who had brought them toward faith. Some followed Paul and others followed Apollos, a gifted speaker and defender of the faith. It's safe to say that neither Paul nor Apollos wanted anything to do with such acclaim. Rather, Paul exhorts them to remember it was God who did it all. In this exhortation, he uses the agricultural metaphor of "planting and watering." Paul played a part (planting), and Apollos played a part (watering). He goes on to say that we are God's fellow workers in this life of witness. God had given

GOD HAD GIVEN EACH THEIR ASSIGNMENT, AND THROUGH THEM GOD WOULD PROMOTE THE GROWTH.

each their assignment, and through them God would promote the growth, leaving God as first witness and us merely cooperators with Him.

Jesus develops the same idea of multiple witnesses in John 4:35–38. In this passage He'd just completed His witness with the woman at the well. She returns to Samaria and tells the village about Jesus. The whole village pours out and heads toward the well to hear and see Jesus for themselves. As the crowd is coming, Jesus says to His disciples:

> *I tell you, open your eyes and look at the fields! They are ripe for harvest. Even now the one who reaps draws a wage and harvests a crop for eternal life, so that the sower and the reaper may be glad together. Thus the saying "One sows and another reaps," is true. . . . Others have done the hard work, and you have reaped the benefits of their labor.*

Jesus tells His disciples that "sowers" and "reapers" have been involved in the saving of many people. In their case, they are about to help bring a whole village to faith in Christ. They are the harvesters, the reapers. Others did the sowing and the watering (1 Corinthians 3).

Taken as a whole, these passages teach us that God uses other believers both together and independently to guide people toward Him. We play different roles in this work—sowing, watering, and reaping. And, just as important, we see that God almost always uses more than one person to help people come to saving faith.

Over the last 35 years, Marie and I have seen God use this pattern to bring many people to Jesus. We've asked, in seminar settings, for Christian people to go back into their memories and ask God to help them recall how many people He brought along-side them in their journey toward Jesus Christ. It's usually about seven to ten unique witnesses!

We've seen it in our own lives. I grew up in a completely irreligious home. My parents weren't against religion, nor were they atheists. They just didn't see much need for the spiritual side of life. They seemed content with what life offered in middle-class America in the 1960s. According to the Barna research group, my parents represented about 11 percent of today's American population (see the book, *The Seven Faith Tribes*, by George Barna). Dad and Mom decided we'd be allowed to make our own choices about religion.

I still remember how strange I felt, however, in the third grade when I realized I was the only kid in my class in Valparaiso, Indiana, that didn't go to church or have religion of some kind. On Mondays at school, it seemed a lot of the kids talked about doing church things on the weekend. I couldn't enter into the stories. But one day, a boy named Bruce, whose dad was a pastor, became my friend. He was a nice boy and became a pretty good friend. Bruce, as I remember, was really kind and fun. He invited me to go to church where his dad served, but I didn't want to go. It felt scary for a third grader with no church background. So I never went. Still, he came to my birthday party and gave me a really, really nice present—a pocketknife. When I think of Bruce, I still smile with gratitude. And that was about 46 years ago!

I don't smile, however, when I think about the next year in that rural Valparaiso school. That's when I learned about the "fear of the Lord." Our teacher in the fourth grade, Mrs. Davidson, was a rather foreboding soul. She could be nice but was more often mean and mad. She referenced God quite a bit, and always with descriptors like "wrathful" or "angry." I especially remember when we had a tornado alert and marched into the basement of the school, where it was cool and dark. Tornadoes weren't very common in our northeast Indiana town, so this was a scary moment for us fourth graders. Mrs. Davidson took the opportunity of such warnings of severe storms to remind us how mad God was at the world and that He could destroy everything at any time He wanted. My limited knowledge of God was developing, I guess. Bruce had displayed the kindness of God, and Mrs. Davidson, the severity. I think to this day she overdid it and nearly terrorized us with her angry portrait of God. A bit of grace would've been nice. We probably behaved better in class without it, though.

My next memory of God using others to show Himself to me occurred in summers. My family vacationed every summer by driving all the way from Indiana to Montana, where our grandparents lived. My mom's parents were pretty religious. They had religious artwork on their farmhouse walls. Grandpa always prayed before we ate. He would take those big, rugged rancher hands and fold them and bow his head to pray. I didn't know what it all meant, but if Grandpa and Grandma were into it, then there was something good about it. As far as I was concerned, if a man rode horses and drove a tractor and believed in God, then God must be real.

About the same time, I guess my mother decided we needed at least a bit of religion, so she taught my brother and me to memorize the Lord's Prayer and recite it at bedtime. I can still see her sitting with me on my single bed with the brown, cowboy bedspread, helping me learn to say the prayer. I knew what some of the words meant but not all of them. For example, "Halloween be thy name," made no sense at all. But as I recall, I prayed the prayer regularly with whatever understanding I had. A year or so later, I made one of the worst mistakes I've ever made when I told my mom that I was too old to have her pray with me. She respected that and never came back in my room to do so. I'd pay whatever the cost to have my mom pray with me today.

In sixth grade, my family moved to California to the beach community of Pacifica. Another boy became my friend, though not as good a friend as Bruce. I don't remember his name, nor his features, but I remember the day he asked if I wanted to go on a church's winter retreat with him. I had no idea what such a thing would be, so I asked him. He told me about snow, lots of girls and boys, sleds, and more. That sounded pretty good, but the idea of the church hosting it was troubling. He told me there would be "talks" about God some of the time too. I was partially put off by that part of it and rather scared.

I'd been at a church one time in my life prior to this, and it was a highly unusual experience. We'd gone to one on Easter a year earlier. The building where God lived was big and dark on the inside with long, wooden benches with no padding. The music was from a huge organ and was weird. The man who talked wore what I thought was a black dress. Yes, the whole religion thing made me wary. It was alien in my imagination. The God notion was more like science fiction than anything.

Well, it got worse. When I told him the next day I didn't want to go, I will never forget his response. He said, "If you don't go on this retreat, you'll probably go to hell." I was scared out of my shoes. I climbed into my mother's arms that night, and even as a big sixth grader cried my eyes out in fear of the devil. It probably also reawakened memories of Mrs. Davidson and Indiana tornado warnings. Mom tried her best to comfort me by saying that God wouldn't do that, but it didn't do much good. Another seed of the "God thing" had been planted in my imaginative mind. I didn't go on the retreat, but I never forgot the boy's words. Those words would be used years later, as I pondered Christianity again. I learned through that experience that God can even use poor or inappropriate witnesses like this boy or Mrs. Davidson to guide people toward Him. Other people tell me the same thing. Isn't our God astounding? He uses even the misguided witnesses in our lives to draw His people toward Himself. It reminds me of something Martin Luther is purported to have said, "The devil is God's devil." God, in His sovereign lordship over the universe, controls and uses everything for His ultimate glory.

From Pacifica we moved to Walnut Creek, California, where I entered middle school. In May of that year, while playing baseball with one of my brothers and friends on the empty street near our home, we heard awful screaming. We threw down our bats and gloves and ran toward the homes where we heard the screaming. As we reached our house, we saw my mother crying out for help and carrying the limp body of my two-year-old brother in her arms. He'd somehow gotten into our backyard and fallen into the swimming pool. He died that night. The sorrow and shock was indescribable. We needed help.

ISN'T OUR GOD ASTOUNDING? HE USES EVEN THE MISGUIDED WITNESSES IN OUR LIVES TO DRAW HIS PEOPLE TOWARD HIMSELF.

Mother called the local Catholic church. Though nonpracticing, she'd been raised Catholic. I am grateful for the two men in "black dresses" who came to us in our sorrows. They led us through the horror of loss and spoke of God and mercy, forgiveness, and the hope of life eternal. It took months to come through the sadness, and in some ways, it is still there. But I will always remember the kind priests who cared for us and spoke to us about God during those treacherous and dark days and months. We went to their church for a couple of years, though not regularly. And though I was confirmed and baptized, we didn't know about the new birth offered to all who call upon Jesus Christ to forgive their sins and place their trust in Him. That was still a few years off for me. Because we had not responded in faith to the gospel, the family soon drifted away from church and spiritual things, as so many casual or nominal Christians do.

Four years later the Christian issue popped up again. In the era of the Beatles and Beach Boys, Bob Dylan, and summer love, I fell hopelessly in love with a girl. My friends told me she went to a Christian youth group and that if I wanted to have any chance with her, I'd better go too. I did. She was there, and the "God thing" was too, only now the God idea was downloaded through a pretty California girl, rock-and-roll music, fun games and skits, and a guy who talked about God as if he knew Him. And he didn't wear a black "dress" like the priests did. I didn't care much about the God stuff as my mind and affections were focused only on the girl . . . at least until she broke up with me for a college man!

The heartbreak of that "lost love" combined with an ongoing and deepening sense of guilt over the death of my brother four years earlier (you see, I was supposed to have been watching him the night he drowned), caused me to start listening to the youth minister talk about God. I went every Tuesday night to the youth group. God used His book as the leader made Jesus come alive and jump off the pages of Scripture. I was drawn to the promise that God would never leave me or forsake me (Hebrews 13:5). God also used the life and words of that youth group leader as well as friends who were loving me and inviting me to know Jesus. I gave what I knew of myself to Christ during the fall of my junior year. I believe He reached down from heaven and, through the lives, love, and voices of many people, drew me to Himself.

I could add other persons who participated in my journey, but that's enough. Bruce, Mrs. Davidson, my grandparents, mom, the sixth grade boy who preached hell, two men in "black dresses," a high school girlfriend, my youth group leader, other friends—God witnessed through them all. As someone once said to me, it takes a village to save a soul. Did you notice that in my long list of people, only three of them were "professionals"? Two Catholic priests and a youth group leader. Most of the witnesses are just average, loving Christians with no theology degrees and no gift of evangelism.

I GAVE WHAT I KNEW OF MYSELF TO CHRIST

I wonder if my story awakens memories in you. Whom did God use to draw you toward Him? Start creating your list now, and expect it to grow over time as God fills in the story of your journey. He will awaken memories and fill you with gratitude. For the most part, I think of these people fondly. God was gracious to me. He sent witnessing souls to stir up a longing for Him within me. *How good is that?*

This truth is vital in effective witness. It takes a lot of pressure off us. We are tempted not only to think we have to save people but also to think we do it alone. Both ideas are wrong. Truthfully, it is stunning to realize that God so loves the world He uses many of us to reach each one. It takes a village.

Now, here's the big question. To whom are we being called today, this week, and this year to sow, water, and reap? Who are our "divine appointments"? I'm glad I don't do it all, but I want to be faithful to do my part.

IT TAKES A VILLAGE

1. God uses many Christians to reach every person. The average we've seen from teaching this principle in many parts of the world is that the majority of Christians identify seven to ten people being used by God in their journey to Jesus.

2. The overwhelming majority of the Christians God uses in the Witness-Life to others are normal, loving believers and not "pros." When we display the truth of this principle in our seminars, people are shocked. We have so identified Witness-Life with ministers, missionaries, or evangelists that we are blown away to find out who really does the bulk of gospel witness. By the way, as one of the so-called pros, I'm really glad to tell all readers that they

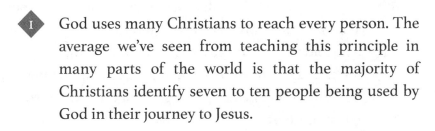

TRUTHFULLY, IT IS STUNNING TO REALIZE THAT GOD SO LOVES THE WORLD HE USES MANY OF US TO REACH EACH ONE.

are more important than they realize and every bit as important as we professionals. It might not make you glad, but I'm tickled. The only way the world will be reached is for multitudes of God's people to engage in the Witness-Life.

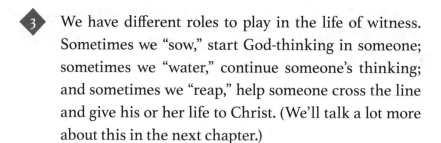

3 We have different roles to play in the life of witness. Sometimes we "sow," start God-thinking in someone; sometimes we "water," continue someone's thinking; and sometimes we "reap," help someone cross the line and give his or her life to Christ. (We'll talk a lot more about this in the next chapter.)

4 God can use misguided witnessing for good ends. Thank God for Mrs. Davidson and the sixth grade boy who told me I would go to hell if I didn't go on his youth retreat. Let's not settle for being misguided witnesses, but how good of God to work through us when we are not at our best.

CHAPTER 3

The One-Step-at-a-Time Journey

ONE of the greatest hindrances to an effective Witness-Life results from a couple of pervasive lies:

LIE #1: We only truly witness when we lead a person all the way to Christ.

LIE #2: (And now, to make it worse.) This spiritual decision should occur in one meeting with a person.

Wrong, on both counts. It can happen in one meeting, but that is quite rare.

Over the last couple of decades, I was privileged to work closely with the Billy Graham Evangelistic Association. One time while talking with their former director of North American crusades, Dr. Sterling Huston, he told me how Mr. Graham would encourage the pastors and leaders of a city as they anticipated an upcoming campaign. I remember he said, "One of the things Mr. Graham always told them was, 'Before I arrive in your city to preach, about 75 percent of the evangelism (witness) is already done.'" Sterling said over the years they realized it was the thousands of Christians in a city who start praying for, caring for, and sharing with friends, relatives, associates, and neighbors that do most of the evangelistic witness. When Mr. Graham arrived, he would preach and call people to the "hour of decision," but for the most part the evangelizing was done before he arrived. Billy Graham understood the "one-step-at-a-time" principle. He saw that finding Christ is a journey for most people, and takes several steps. If this is the case, and I wholeheartedly believe it is, then where did the lies come from?

I believe these lies originated from two eras in evangelical history, especially in America, and the two modalities that shaped the view of evangelical witness. The first model started in the early twentieth century when mass public evangelism and immediately publicized results became so popular. The work of Billy Sunday best typifies this model. His public meetings in both large cities and rural towns of America brought great attention to the power of the gospel. The crowds grew so large and the respondents so numerous that expediency finally led him to declare that a prayer uttered by a listener at the time of the invitation all but guaranteed the impartation of salvation. The size of the crowds and lack of available counselors led Sunday's organization to discontinue face-to-face meetings with inquirers as evangelist Dwight L. Moody had done before him. Of course, this regretfully took away the opportunity for mature believers to immediately find out what was transpiring in the soul of the person.

Billy Graham and a host of others followed the Billy Sunday model of public prayer meetings signifying that something regenerative was happening in the lives of the listeners. It must be noted, however, Mr. Graham and his team did not equate a spiritual decision in his meetings with the moment of salvation. That is why he always called those who came forward "inquirers." In fact, the level of personal follow-up provided to every inquirer by the Graham Association is exemplary and, in my opinion, the best practice for all mass evangelism occurring today. Yet, most Christians who attended and saw the gigantic responses did equate the events with immediate regeneration. The die was cast. American evangelicalism began to see evangelism and witness as achieving a faith decision resulting in salvation in one fell swoop.

The second model became popular as I was growing up in the 1960s, during which I became a Christ follower and almost immediately began sharing my faith. This era accompanied the "Jesus Movement," which I remember impacted a generation of young people coinciding with the social cataclysm of the 60s and 70s. By and large this model was practiced by the parachurch groups God raised up following World War II to assist local churches in Witness-Life.

Bill Bright and Campus Crusade for Christ (now called Cru) created the *Four Spiritual Laws* booklet and urged staff and students on campuses all over America to share the booklet with a curious listener and call for a prayer of commitment at the end. Other groups did similar things. Again, I don't believe Mr.

WITNESS OCCURS WHENEVER A CHRIST-FOLLOWER ENABLES A CURIOUS PERSON TO UNDERSTAND A BIT MORE, TO EDGE A BIT CLOSER TO GOD AND HIS GRACE.

Bright, Campus Crusade, nor other parachurch groups equated the prayer with a guaranteed secured salvation, but as with Mr. Graham and his organization, it began to be interpreted that way by the majority of evangelicals.

Today many evangelicals still believe the "sinner's prayer," prayed in the first discussion with a person about God, provides the assurance of salvation. While regeneration may indeed happen at such an occasion, it is only validated as time goes on and the life of the inquirer begins changing. It is not my intention to right this wrong; I have dealt with it more extensively in the book *Going Public with the Gospel,* which I coauthored with Mark Anderson.

These "lies," or assumptions, hinder most of God's people from realizing they practice the Witness-Life whenever they share anything about Jesus Christ with a listener. Witness occurs whenever a Christ-follower enables a curious person to understand a bit more, to edge a bit closer to God and His grace. Let me revisit our definition and hone our focus on the final phrase. The Witness-Life is, "to cooperate with God and others, to lovingly bring people one step at a time closer to God." Finding God is more of a journey than a one-step event. Remember our discussion in chapter 2 emphasizing the many believers God uses to bring a person to Himself? We referenced the passages from 1 Corinthians 3 and John 4, in which Paul and Jesus describe the journey to God through the agricultural picture of sowing, watering, and reaping. That imagery describes it perfectly. That truth shows how the process of coming to God is a journey or series of events and encounters as God uses people, nature, art, life longings, and struggles to guide people a step at a time toward Christ.

I remember our neighbor John, who came to Christ through a series of steps. John and Kate moved into our neighborhood in the Chicago suburbs a couple of years after we did. It was our practice then, as now, to invite new neighbors into our home as soon as possible to welcome them to the community, help in any way we can with their adjustment, and, as God directs, start a prayerful Witness-Life with them if they are open to it. They came to dinner one night. In our dining room, we had some Christian art, most notably, a portrait of Jesus with all creation gathered around Him in beautiful harmony. Trees, a running brook, animals, and people all surrounded Jesus in the picture. The picture led John to ask about my career path. So in front of my children and his son, I told him I was a Christian minister and traveled around the country helping people who were looking for God. That led to a couple of questions from John, but essentially that was the first step.

We spent other times talking with John, Kate, and their son. We raked leaves together. We shot the breeze in the autumn days. One day John said he'd been at a funeral in a church and had a couple of questions. So, we talked. At some point Marie talked with John and Kate too. I don't remember the content of our many discussions. Sometimes we spoke of our faith, and other times it just wasn't appropriate to do so (more later on how to discern spiritual openness).

Then a time came when I sensed a real spiritual curiosity in John. The Holy Spirit was working in him and allowed us to see it. He knew very little about God, Jesus, or the Bible. I asked if he liked to read books to which he responded, "not much." Then I asked if he liked movies to which he said, "yes." So, we lent him our copy of the *Jesus* film. Time went on. I didn't know if he watched it or not.

One day while we were talking John said, "Hey, Lon, I didn't know Jesus got ticked off." Sure enough, he had watched the film and the scene of Jesus clearing the temple of those buying and selling goods really got to him. John related to Jesus' anger! Who would have thought that would be a path into John's life? But it was. More discussions over time ensued. I think we invited John and his family to our newly forming church, but I don't think they came.

As time passed, we noticed there were problems next door with John and Kate. They weren't around as much. I'm sure I wondered if I'd pushed too hard with the spiritual questions leading them to withdraw. But in reality it was other things. You see, they weren't married, and their son was really just Kate's son. Being a blended family can be hard and terribly difficult when there is not the commitment of marriage led by Jesus Christ. Sure enough, parenting differences led them to split. John moved out. Kate didn't say much. Months passed. Then one day there was a knock on the door. It was John. We were so glad to see him and welcomed him warmly. He then asked if he could talk to me. I assumed he wanted my help to try and reconcile with Kate. But no, that wasn't it at all. He told me that during the course of his struggles, he realized he needed God badly. I was out of town, so he went to the Lutheran church where he had gone to the funeral, and the pastor met with him and guided him to place his faith in Jesus Christ. John was born again! He had come to our house because the pastor told him he should tell others about his new faith in Christ. Marie joined me in the meeting with John that day. We prayed, and I think maybe wept together with joy. John was already displaying the first fruits of true conversion. He was peaceful, full of gratitude, and in love with God that day in our living room.

I don't remember ever seeing John again. He moved to another area. We continued to reach out to Kate, and over time, sure enough, she and her son returned to the church of her childhood. They played on our church coed softball team and were in fellowship with our church whenever events were held at our house. Her conversion was not as sudden as John's, but it came nonetheless, over time and through a series of events. She too became a child of God.

John and Kate exemplify the way most people come to faith, one step at a time. God used friendship, art, film, the Bible, gospel discussion, and crisis over the period of a year or longer to secure John's salvation. Kate came to faith through crisis, friendship, a local church fellowship, the church of her childhood, and only God knows what else.

All of this experience begs the question, do we see this concept of "one step at a time closer" in Scripture? In the New Testament we don't receive the details of a person's journey toward Christ. If anything, most of the narratives in the Gospels and the Book of Acts make it appear that belief and conversion happen immediately and fully. For instance, in the beginning of Acts, Peter preaches the first sermon, and 3,000 come to faith that very day (Acts 2:41). But, look a bit deeper. Those 3,000 were Jews from all over the world in Jerusalem for Pentecost, worshipping God to the degree they knew Him. It was a deeply spiritual time for them. They had journeyed to Jerusalem, praying each day to grow closer to God. Then the Holy Spirit started preaching the "wonders of God" (Acts 2:11) to them in their own heart languages. Following the Spirit's direct message, Peter preached. Then they came to faith. It was a journey—one step at a time closer—and if one considers the travel the Jews from all over the world had made to get to Jerusalem, this process had been going on for months, perhaps most of their lives, as they worshipped the God of their history!

Here's another example. Jesus sees Andrew and Simon (soon to be Peter) fishing in Galilee. He simply says, "'Come, follow me, ... and I will send you out to fish for people.' At once, they left their nets and followed him" (Mark 1:17–18). It looks like their conversion was immediate and life changing. Yet even in this case, if we look to another Gospel where Andrew and Simon are called (John 1:26–42), it appears there are steps to the story that occur before Jesus calls them out of the boat. Andrew was a follower of John the Baptist before he met Jesus. This suggests that Andrew was in a period of spiritual searching and had found John to be a guide on his journey. John is in Bethany at the Jordan River near Jerusalem, where he baptizes Jesus. John declares that Jesus is the Lamb of God in the hearing of Andrew. He actually tells him twice, once publicly and then the next day semiprivately (John 1:29, 35–36).

Andrew starts to follow Jesus and spends a period of time with Him, probably several days as Jesus heads north to Galilee. By the time they get to Galilee, Andrew has come to believe Jesus is the Messiah. Then Andrew goes to find Peter, who is in another place, and brings him to meet Jesus. It appears that only after these events, perhaps as soon as the next day, Jesus calls Andrew and Peter from the fishing boat. So again, even with John the Baptist and Jesus present, it appears the movement of Andrew and Peter to Jesus was a journey.

The conversion of the Apostle Paul is another compelling case for the "one step at a time closer" concept. A careful look at Acts and two of Paul's letters tells the story. Like Andrew and like the Jews in Jerusalem at Pentecost, Paul displays spiritual hunger when we meet him. He studies with a premier Jewish scholar, the Pharisee Gamaliel (Acts 5:34; 22:3), and becomes a Pharisee like him. Paul is passionate for his faith in Yahweh (Galatians 1:14). He tries to please God through a rigorous commitment to obedience and good works (Philippians 3:6). He hears the gospel of Jesus Christ preached by Stephen and is not impressed. He goes ballistic. When the followers of Jesus suggest to Paul that his Jewish faith is incomplete, he joins a mob to kill the Christian preacher (Acts 7:57–60). He then makes it his life calling to stop all Christians by force and incarceration (Acts 8:1–3). He even takes a job working under the authority of Jewish religious leaders to root out the false sect (Christians) throughout Israel (Acts 9:1–2).

During all of this he finally faces the truth after receiving a vision of Jesus, one that blinds him and stops him in his tracks (vv. 4–6). He faces Jesus in his blindness and hears His voice, much like the stories we hear of many Muslim people in unreached parts of the world today. While Paul remains blind in Damascus for three days, the Lord reveals himself to a Christian named Ananias. The Lord tells Ananias to speak to Paul about Christ and heal his blindness (vv. 10–16). Then Paul is baptized as a follower of Jesus (v. 18). This whole process—from seeking God through his early Jewish faith to finding Jesus—took years. It would be another three years or more before he was fully ready to preach Christ and reach the world with the Jesus story (Galatians 1:18).

EVERY TIME YOU DISPLAY YOUR FAITH THROUGH ACTS OF KINDNESS OR JUSTICE AND EXPLAIN WHY YOU ARE DOING SO, YOU ARE PRACTICING WITNESS-LIFE.

Every time you pray for a person to be saved, you are practicing Witness-Life. Every time you display your faith through acts of kindness or justice and explain why you are doing so, you are practicing Witness-Life. Every time you offer a blessing to a neighbor, ask a restaurant server how you can pray for them, or send a note to a colleague with a salutation of blessing, you are practicing Witness-Life. Every time you share the story of how God found you and forgave you, you are practicing Witness-Life. Finally, whenever you have the privilege of praying with a person to commit to Christ, you are practicing Witness-Life. It's all Witness-Life, as the First Witness mysteriously draws people to Himself through a journey only He knows from beginning to end.

The journey of one step at a time closer cannot be plotted with specificity on a time line, but there are some general signposts I've noticed as the journey unwinds. I am indebted to the work of some leading missions and communications scholars from the 1970s who, as far as I know, started to define the steps toward faith in Christ and place them in a somewhat determinate continuum.

James Engel was the coordinator and early creator of this idea. He and Wil Norton wrote about it in their book, *What's Gone Wrong with the Harvest?* Since then, many adaptations of it have been suggested. Marie and I have attempted to take the Engel continuum and add a stronger relational dimension to it. For this I have also borrowed from the good work of Don Everts and Doug Schaupp in their book, *I Once Was Lost.* My 46 years of experience tells me that almost everyone who journeys to faith in Jesus has people (believers) involved all along the way. I have crafted the continuum to include that reality and hopefully make it more understandable and applicable for the believer seeking to help someone they know come one or many steps closer to Christ. Marie and I call this the modified relational-Engel scale. Before you read further, please take a minute to look at the chart on page 64 and 65. I'm always tempted to skip the charts in a book and jump down to the next paragraph of text. Don't do that with this one—big mistake. I promise it will be worth your time.

TRUST

The chart chronicles a person's faith journey, which begins with the first stages of trust as the person goes about their own way living life without God (-12). The person may be an atheist or a secularist who affirms a belief in God's existence but has little or no connection with Him or evident need for Him. Such a person might also be someone who believes in a god other than our Christian understanding of God. Recalling that God uses believers to participate in His calling of lost souls, believers are brought into the person's life (-11). It might be just one believer, and they start to like that person. They see a little Christlike character in the person and are naturally attracted. This has happened for us whenever we've moved into a new neighborhood over the last 37 years! It's not only my wife and me who live in the neighborhood, however. Jesus has moved in as well, dwelling in us and beginning the divine mystery of drawing us into people's lives. Our addresses at home, work, and in our community have been chosen for us by God. He intends to not only be with us in all our life matters but also He ordains our connections with people who don't know Him. With God's guidance the person begins to trust the Christ follower and starts to notice qualitative differences in the life of the Christian (-10, -9). This happened in our relationships with John and Kate.

CURIOUS

While we do life with the person, God works inside his or her life and awakens awareness of personal needs as they move from the trust stage to the curious stage. This is a kind of disequilibrium (-8). Sometimes these needs are very apparent to those on the

✳ ONE STEP CLOSER TO CHRIST ✳
SPIRITUAL JOURNEY

This modified relational-Engel scale gives a general sense of the stages people move through as they journey toward Christ.

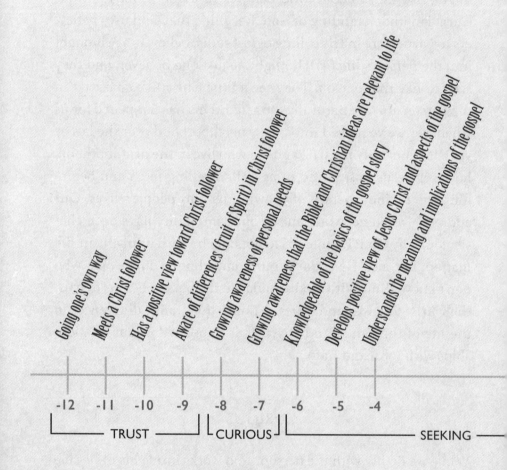

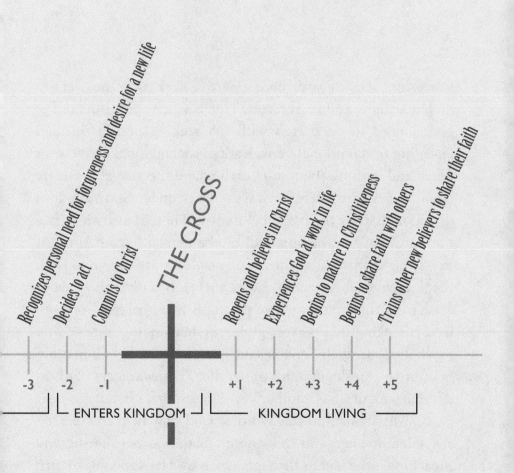

THE CROSS

Recognizes personal need for forgiveness and desire for a new life

Decides to act

Commits to Christ

Repents and believes in Christ

Experiences God at work in life

Begins to mature in Christlikeness

Begins to share faith with others

Trains other new believers to share their faith

-3   -2   -1   +1   +2   +3   +4   +5

ENTERS KINGDOM   KINGDOM LIVING

outside, like a loss of job or a close relationship. Other times friends and neighbors won't have any idea the disequilibrium exists. But it is this unsettledness that opens more curiosity to the idea, and maybe even the hope, of a God who is personal and might be able to help. In God's goodness, He has brought believers into the person's life and often has already sown gospel seeds through the sharing of life, stories, and ideas that correspond to a Christ-centered worldview. And now, these ideas start making sense (-7).

SEEKING

Curiosity turns toward more assertive seeking of answers to life's questions and its sorrows. This is when the truths of the gospel need to be shared with the seeking person through engaging in intentional conversation, sharing books, tracts, or films, and inviting them to church where the gospel is clearly taught. These are just a few ways to work under God's gracious direction to draw the person closer (-6). There is also an attraction to Christ that begins to draw the person toward Him. At first he or she liked the Christian, now they are drawn to God, the Source of all goodness and peace (-5). Usually, things accelerate from this point on. The person is now seeking God, and God is seeking that person, giving understanding of need and much more. God also enables the person to see that all manner of disorder is resident in his or her life. This awareness of disorder that we call sin is another key signpost that salvation is near (-4, -3). Christians and the Word of God now help this person see a decision can and needs to be made. Gospel sharing and preaching is the means through which God leads people to turn away from or repent of self-leadership and all manner of sin and turn to God's gracious acceptance and direction.

ENTERS KINGDOM

In the mystery of God, at His perfect moment, the seeker is drawn from darkness to light and is born anew spiritually (-2). God joins His life with the seeker's life, and a new birth occurs (-1) in the person's spirit by the Holy Spirit (2 Corinthians 5:17). Joy of joys. With the angels we soar whenever a person turns to God (Luke 15).

Above my desk hangs a picture by the artist Ron DiCianni of two angels dressed in white. They appear to be young men in their twenties or thirties. Their faces peer down over a white railing, giving the sense of watching earth from heaven, exuding joy and wonder. They are laughing uproariously. I'm pretty sure it is Ron's rendition of our Lord's words, "I tell you, there is rejoicing in the presence of the angels of God over one sinner who repents" (Luke 15:10). There really is. I've had that joy, and I bet you have too. My heart cries out for us all in prayer, "Oh, God, allow us the privilege of that kind of joy more often!"

KINGDOM LIVING

The modified relational-Engel scale doesn't end at the new birth because the journey is not over. Obstetrics moves aside, and pediatrics begins. God ordains this next portion of the person's development, once again utilizing believers to walk with the person as Christ is formed in them (+1 to +5). This is the never-ending story for all believers as long as we live on earth. Can you remember your new birth? Do you remember the saints God used as obstetricians and those He used and uses still in the pediatrics? Sometimes they are the same person!

Let me return to our definition of the Witness-Life. "To cooperate with God and others to lead a person one step at a time closer to Christ." We've discussed the three big ideas in the definition, namely: God is the evangelist; it takes a village to save a soul—He uses many believers in each seeker's life; and one step closer—the new birth is generally the result of a journey, one step at a time.

There is one additional caveat I want to discuss at this juncture. Sometimes the one step at a time closer journey ends up being more of a "one step forward, two steps back," or at least it can seem like it. People often start on the path of searching for God but seem to hit barriers or roadblocks along the way. Jim Petersen, in the "Evangelism as a Lifestyle" drama and video series, writes of this. He suggests four distinct roadblocks. Let me illustrate.

SPIRITUAL ROADBLOCK

Shari has a cousin named Alice who moved from Montana to Philadelphia. They'd not known each other much growing up, but now, as young adults, living in the same city and only one neighborhood apart, they could start a friendship. Shari found Christ as a little girl in a Backyard Bible Club and from that time at age six had always sensed the nearness of God and loved Jesus. So it was natural for her to share that part of her life with Alice.

Alice was raised in the land of mountains, Grizzlies football, and cowboys. Philadelphia was exciting and only a bit frightening to her. After all, there were more people in the city of

Philadelphia than in the whole state of Montana. She was counting on Shari to help her learn about the new exciting world of urban America. She was enthralled by it. She wanted to visit downtown clubs and museums and the Liberty Bell and drive up to New York City. She had no interest whatsoever in spiritual things. Whenever Shari said anything about her faith, Alice's eyes glazed over. She was polite but not interested.

This is a spiritual roadblock. Jesus made it clear that many people would be attracted to all the things of this world at the exclusion of spiritual matters. We see this mostly in the developed countries of the world, where, as Jesus said, "the deceitfulness of wealth and the desire for other things . . . choke the word, making it unfruitful" (Mark 4:19). The world's allure had a hold on Alice, quite strongly. And we know that Satan was fueling the whole thing. Paul tells us, "The god of this age has blinded the minds of unbelievers, so that they cannot see the light of the gospel" (2 Corinthians 4:4).

EMOTIONAL ROADBLOCK

Tom began asking Jim a few questions about God after they played tennis one morning. Jim had been praying for Tom for a couple of years, had shared the story of his life and finding Jesus, and generally enjoyed their time on the court and the smoothies that followed in the café. Their friendship grew as each shared more and more meaningful things with the other. That's why Jim wasn't too surprised that God came up that day.

For the next couple of weeks, Tom asked more questions and seemed curious, but then it all stopped suddenly. It stopped the day he asked Jim about getting to heaven and how a person could be sure they were going there. Before Jim could respond, Tom said, "All I know for sure is that if there is a heaven, then both my parents are there because they were two of the best people you could imagine." That's when Jim said as carefully as he knew how, "Well the Bible is pretty clear that our goodness has nothing to do with getting to heaven." He went on to talk about the fact that compared to God none of us are very good and that we all needed forgiveness. Tom brought the conversation to a halt and said, "If your God doesn't have room for my parents, I want nothing to do with Him!" For weeks to follow, Tom and Jim didn't talk about God, and in fact, they didn't talk at all.

This is an example of the emotional roadblock. Tom couldn't objectively listen to any idea that suggested even remotely that his parents could be excluded from heaven. He wouldn't listen any longer. Jim wanted badly to talk further. He wanted badly to help Tom understand that God's goodness is so immense it provides forgiveness for all our badness if we admit we are all tainted by evil and need God. But the emotional barrier shut down all chance of that discussion. There was still hope, but it would take time and lots of prayer to rebuild some trust for Tom to listen to Jim.

INTELLECTUAL ROADBLOCK

Franklin is a scientist, and by everyone's accounts, a good one. He'd worked at Lawrence Livermore National Laboratory for a decade after graduating from the California Institute of Technology in physics. He is also a good guy, and unless you asked him about his work, he wouldn't bore anyone with the latest theory of particle physics. He could eat corn chips and cheer on the Golden State Warriors as much as the next fan, unless you got him going on the physics behind Stephen Curry's three-point acumen.

Franklin is a smart, decent guy who lives alone in his Livermore townhome next door to Felicia and Nora, who (can you guess?) both love Jesus. They love the Warriors too, and the cheering coming from their unit on game nights (not to mention their good looks) brought Franklin (not shy about his own "way with the ladies") to knock at their door one evening and ask them over to watch the game. Basketball, chips, drinks, good-natured flirting, and neighborly help with a circuit breaker and short in the microwave also got him invited into their home more than once.

The ladies got up the nerve to invite Franklin to join them at their church sometime. He was respectful but declined saying, "I'm sorry, but I don't even believe there is a God. So you really don't want me there." And then, because he was a good guy he said, "I hope I've not offended you. I just don't see life through that lens, and I hope that doesn't hinder our friendship." It didn't hurt the friendship, and over time Felicia and Nora, who were both social workers, learned more about Franklin's scientific objections to the Christian faith. Step by step they were willing to be honest friends and pray for an open door to his mind and heart. This is the intellectual roadblock.

VOLITIONAL ROADBLOCK

Orion was a university-educated, first-generation immigrant from Albania. He remembered the Iron Curtain and the repression of that time when he was a boy. As political tyranny ended in his atheistic country, his parents encouraged him to "do better" than they'd been allowed to do. At an early age, they planted the seed in him—a desire to go to America. He was one of the fortunate ones who did, and when he arrived, his visa in hand, he thought he was the luckiest man in the world. His goal was to find good work in the engineering field and make a way to bring his two brothers and sister to America as soon as possible. He knew he made his parents proud. Their dream had been for Orion, as the oldest, to get a degree, get out, and provide the means for his siblings to follow.

He didn't know anyone in the United States. But he used his education and hard work ethic to find volunteer-based organizations that helped immigrants adjust. That's where he met Stewart. Stewart was a volunteer at an agency and helped Orion find lodging, a job, and even helped him with his legal documents. They would often have coffee together and went to dinner a time or two. Orion was deeply impressed by Stewart, who volunteered to help immigrants like himself. As he learned more of his advocate's life, he found out he was also a—you guessed it—Christian. Stewart told Orion that Jesus Christ had been an immigrant and, in fact, a refugee. He told him that Jesus taught His followers to do good to all people. He told him it was because of Jesus that he volunteered to help people like Orion. Orion was intrigued and was drawn first to Stewart and then to Stewart's Jesus.

Within a couple of months, he started going to Stewart's church and even hung out with a group of single adults who did a lot together beyond church. One of Stewart's friends told Orion about a group that was designed for people wanting to know more about God. He loved it. He listened intently. He asked lots of questions. He wanted to get closer to God until Stewart dropped "the lordship bomb" on him. Stewart told him that knowing God and Jesus included giving over the control of his life to Jesus. That stopped him in his tracks. He had come from a place where trust in authority was nonexistent. He'd been taught by his parents to make something of his life, to learn everything he could, and to work hard. He wanted the American dream. He had a plan to help his family come to the United States. He had a plan to become an electrical engineer with a large company. The notion of needing to lay his plans aside if God had a different one was unfathomable for him. He would not and could not give his future or that of his family to anyone else, not even the Christian God. This is the volitional roadblock.

Being aware of the roadblock (or roadblocks, as sometimes the person we are witnessing to has more than one) allows us to pray more effectively and better prepare to reach our friend. One of the persons I've shared with for over three years now has a scientific mind and PhD to prove it. I really love the guy, and we cherish him and his mother also, until her recent death. I've learned that his intellectual questions about Christianity, while real, seem less of an issue than his will (volition). One time he responded, "I know what you are asking me to do. I know what it means. It means giving over the control of my life. I'm not ready for that." My prayers for him grew from asking God to open his eyes to things he can't see and prove to also doing whatever it takes to convince him he needs divine leadership to make life work.

I hope I've not scared any readers with the four stories above. The roadblocks are real but not as real as the risen Lord Jesus Christ. All things are possible with God. Remember, God loves everyone as if they were the only one, and ultimately, He is the evangelist. He uses a posse of people to help each honestly seeking person find Him. It is a step at a time, and even a step backwards is not a problem for a seeking God who knows every way around every roadblock! He can and does shatter the roadblocks.

THE ROADBLOCKS ARE REAL BUT NOT AS REAL AS THE RISEN LORD JESUS CHRIST.

How do we cooperate with God and others to lovingly bring people like Tom, Alice, Franklin, and Orion one step at a time closer to Christ? *Aha!* Now, I'm really excited. Why? Because I now get to teach you the wonderful Prayer, Care, Share model of the Witness-Life. I can hardly wait. Keep the three Witness-Life truths we've just discussed close to you as we proceed. They were the appetizers before the main course.

CHAPTER 4

Learning to Enjoy the Witness-Life
Prayer, Care, and Share

A FEW years ago a friend asked if I wanted to go on a "great adventure."

"What do you have in mind?" I asked.

"Let's climb a big mountain," he said.

I don't remember how long we discussed it, but in the end I said, "Yes!"

Now, to climb a large mountain you must be in pretty good shape. Little did I know that we had chosen what many call the hardest mountain in the lower 48 states—Mount Rainier in the state of Washington. It is 14,411 feet high, which makes it difficult, but there are many 14-ers in the United States. So why, you might ask, is Mount Rainier the toughest? Good question. The answer is because of its many glaciers. That fact alone raised a red flag—was I fit enough in my midfifties to do it? But, I wasn't really worried. Fitness is a hobby of mine. I've been involved in fitness conditioning for nearly my whole life! Mostly, I've lifted weights.

My friend Peter was really fit. Compared to him I was a novice. He was, by education, a professor of health science. His body was and still is his laboratory, and not so long ago he competed in USA Powerlifting's national competition and was named the strongest man in America for his age category. He told me in no uncertain terms that we must become more than good weightlifters to climb Mount Rainier. We needed to focus on specific regions in our backs, legs, and ankles, and we must elevate our cardiovascular fitness because of how quickly we were going into thin air. So he put together a cross-training regimen for us, strengthening all four of those areas.

In the end, we made the climb, and both of us finished the ascent and descent in the very quick two-day time period allowed. God helped us, and to this day, I say it was the toughest physical thing I've ever done. I wouldn't have made it without the cross-training that worked the different regions of my body to get me ready.

The Witness-Life also requires cross-training. Most people hear the terms *evangelize* or *witness*, and they immediately think of one thing—talking to someone about Jesus Christ. They are right but not completely right. Why? Because it takes more than just talking or sharing verbally. It takes praying, caring (loving beyond the expected), and sharing. That's where I get the easily remembered themes of Prayer, Care, and Share.

I remember when the rhymed words of *prayer, care,* and *share* came together for me. It was 1991. Wow, that seems a long time ago. I'd just begun serving a denomination, the Evangelical Covenant Church, and was their director of evangelism. Before taking the position, I'd been studying several different approaches to personal evangelism and wanted to find a way to concisely and compellingly teach it to my local church members. The approaches usually emphasized the importance of praying and the value of loving people in extraordinary ways. Then they taught about the importance of talking or telling others about Jesus. So, prayer, loving, and talking were all vital. I worked hard to teach them to my congregation.

Fast-forward to my new calling. I'm now the pied piper of

evangelism for a whole denomination. It's no longer just one congregation but hundreds. How could I help teach and inspire them all to step into the Witness-Life? One day at a national denominational meeting I was chatting with my pastor friend Randy about my dilemma. I told him about the three aspects of witness—praying, loving, and talking. He concurred. But then I said, "Randy, I need to find a way to clearly and compellingly teach the truths with memorable language. That's essential for it to catch on in our denominational family of churches." He agreed. So together, in the hotel lobby, we brainstormed. And that is when the words *prayer, care,* and *share* came to us. I know this seems simplistic, but I honestly believe God inspired us in that lobby in Chicago in the winter of 1991 because the terms work so well to help people grasp the three big themes of sharing faith. Now, more than 25 years later, I see and hear the terms used by so many people in so many church and parachurch settings. It's a deep joy to know Randy and I had a little bit to do with the whole thing when God helped us find the words, *prayer, care,* and *share.*

I hope they will stick well for you too. I'd like to make the case that these themes are the three biblically affirmed actions of the Witness-Life. Additionally, effective Witness-Life requires two key attitudes—*courage* and *perseverance.* To tie those attitudes into the formula, I continue the rhyming convention with *dare* and for the second, (this one is really a stretch), *hanging in there.* Three actions—*prayer, care,* and *share*—undergirded with two attitudes—*dare* and *hanging in there.* I hope this doesn't come across as either too simplistic or complex. In actuality, it is very freeing to realize that all three of the actions are witnessing, and each needs the others. Just as being physically fit requires the conditioning of all the regions of the body, so too the Witness-Life requires the three actions undergirded by the two attitudes. Here's what it looks like visually.

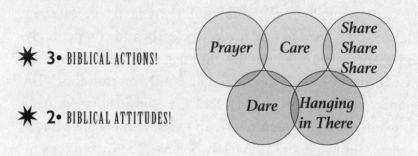

✳ 3• BIBLICAL ACTIONS!

✳ 2• BIBLICAL ATTITUDES!

While on our Mount Rainier expedition, we needed a guide. It was too technical of a climb to scale without a professional, to whom we were tethered by rope, to guide us every step of the way. The same holds for the Witness-Life. Jesus Christ is our example, and even more importantly, our hands-on guide Who will be with us every step of the way in every Witness-Life adventure we have. Remember, He is the evangelist. So, let's get into our training and start the great adventure!

JESUS CHRIST IS OUR EXAMPLE, AND EVEN MORE IMPORTANTLY, OUR HANDS-ON GUIDE.

STARTING POINT

Just before we begin our Witness-Life training, it will be helpful to do a bit of a self-assessment. We need to be honest with ourselves about where we are at the start of our preparation. Look at the following Witness-Life thermometer, and gauge where you see yourself right now. Are you cold, warm, or getting hot? Wherever you are, here is the good news: God wants to guide you to become warmer. If, after you read the descriptors, you honestly place yourself as cold, that's where you start. If you see yourself in the warm or hot range, so be it. Wherever you start, that's not where you are going to end. You're going to get a lot hotter!

✳ WITNESS-LIFE THERMOMETER ✳

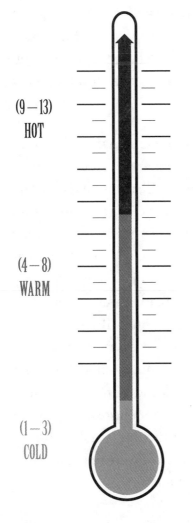

(9 – 13)
HOT

(4 – 8)
WARM

(1 – 3)
COLD

• I am knowledgeable of His story, the gospel, and anxious to share it!

• I have regular opportunities to start God-talk with people.

• I have written out my story and am ready to tell it at any time.

• I have non-Christian friends and invite them to events where Jesus is shared regularly.

• I am disciplined about praying for people to be saved.

• I find God reminding me to pray for people, and I obey sometimes.

• I often think of things I wish I had said to people about God.

• I love hearing stories of people finding God.

• I think about witnessing occasionally and feel guilty that I don't do it much.

• I'm starting to look for opportunities to care for and share with others.

• I never, or very seldom, think about witnessing.

• Witnessing is for pastors/evangelists, not me.

• I'm too busy managing everything else in my life.

I remember when my fitness-climbing friend, Peter, told me we were not in good enough shape to climb Mount Ranier. We had to strengthen our quadriceps (thighs) and cardiovascular fitness significantly to make the climb. He told me to do so we were going to go up and down stadium steps at our college's football field. So, we did. I was somewhat pleased at my pace and endurance for the first few attempts, at least at first. I would have rated myself at about a 5 on the thermometer. Then he said, "Now we're going to build up to doing it without stopping for 45 minutes." *Uh-oh.* You guessed it. I was plumb tuckered out. But I built up to it as I practiced. From there we added backpacks and 40 pounds of weight. You guessed it. Another *uh-oh.* But again, learning the technique and practice paid off, and I got stronger. By the end, the whole thing started to feel natural. It was like my body was made for it.

WOULDN'T IT BE WONDERFUL IF WE BECAME AS COMMITTED, TRAINED, AND EXPERIENCED IN WITNESS-LIFE AS WE ARE AT READING THE BIBLE, STUDYING SCRIPTURE, OR WORSHIPPING IN GOD'S HOUSE?

It's the same with the Witness-Life. Wherever you are measuring, you will, through technique and practice, get better and better. Now someone reading this may say, "I've looked at the thermometer. And I don't want to brag, but I'm already pretty hot." My answer? Get hotter. If you are a 10, go to 11. "From everyone who has been given much, much will be demanded" (Luke 12:48). Wouldn't it be wonderful if we became as committed, trained, and experienced in Witness-Life as we are at reading the Bible, studying Scripture, or worshipping in God's house? We can be, and we will be. We were made for this. So, where do you start on the thermometer?

OK. I think we are ready. We've taken our temperature. We have a goal: to enjoy and become effective in the Witness-Life. We know where we are starting. We are ready to learn the three actions and two attitudes and enter into a great adventure!

CHAPTER 5

Prayer-Witness

WHEN I learned prayer is an essential action and requirement in the Witness-Life, a light turned on for me.

Early in our ministry, when my wife and I were planting our second church in Northern California, I felt like a failure. Our first church plant was staggeringly successful, but our second one was a slow, long process over time. Compared to our first experience, it seemed almost a disaster. I didn't know why.

You see, when we started our first church, I didn't know how to do it. I read some books and clung tightly to the mentor-leader from my denomination helping me. He told me he wasn't very good at it either, but together we'd trust God and give it our best. I was only 25, with little theological education and only a few years of experience as a youth director. But God showed up big time. Sixteen people a week became 800 people a week within four years. Even better, hundreds of those people came to faith in Christ through that church. It met in an X-rated-movie theatre, so it wasn't the building that brought the folks. I was just learning to preach, and more, I was too young to know much about life, so, for sure, it wasn't my eloquence or wisdom. Vestiges of the Jesus Movement, however, still had a slippery grip on the West Coast. That may've been part of the reason it succeeded. I'll never know.

Here's the point. The second church we planted should have been even more successful. After all, I now had a degree in theology, and I'd taken courses in church growth and evangelism. I had been preaching for many years and had training and more experience. The worship team was super, and Marie and I were smarter and more mature. But, as I said, it languished. Six years in, we still hadn't broken 200 attendees. What was it? "Why, God?" I asked. I didn't know if that prayer would be tangibly answered. I probably didn't think it would be. But it was.

One day I was driving from our area to Sacramento, which was about a 90-minute trip. As I passed through the famous San Joaquin Valley, considered one of the richest farmlands in the world, I prayed and poured out my sadness and confusion about our church to God. I just couldn't make it work. Since the first church had been so successful, I was considered somewhat of a wonder kid in reaching people for Jesus. That made the slowness of the second church even harder and more embarrassing, because my ambition and ego were taking a shot. (By the way—that was a good thing, a very good thing!)

As I prayed I had one of those rare moments in which God spoke to me through a vision, or an image. I don't get those often, but when I do they impact me. I'll never ever forget it. The whole thing probably lasted no more than a minute, but, boy, did it have power. I saw an image of a giant hand, and in the hand was a large dirt clod. The clod was as hard as a rock. Nothing could break it apart. It was like stone. Then, a gentle rain began to fall on the clod, and slowly the clod softened and became pliable. That was it. That was the whole thing. I had no idea what it meant. But the image was strong and as long-lasting, as those rare words from God often are.

About a week later I was with some of the men in our church on a retreat in the Sierra Nevada Mountains. Late on that Friday night, about 20 of us went into a time of very deep and honest worship and sharing. I decided I'd tell the guys about my mysterious "dirt clod" vision. I was taking a chance. Some of these guys were new Christians or not-yet Christians. Some were Christians from pretty conservative backgrounds. I was clearly in danger of being labeled the weird pastor. I shared it anyway. I didn't get much response, as I recall, at least not to my face.

But after everyone had gone to bed, one of the men came up to me quietly and said something like, "I don't know if this is real or not, but as you were sharing the story of your vision, I felt like God was saying something to me."

"What was it?" I asked.

"Well," he said, "I think God told me the dirt clod is the hard ground on which we are trying to grow our church." He went on, "and the gentle rain, I think, is prayer."

He was one of the most mature believers in our church and a trustworthy friend. All I remember for sure is that everything in my spirit leaned into sensing truth in those words.

I felt like God was confirming the vision through this friend. It shook me and radically changed me from a church-growth wonder kid who felt he was failing to a humble young leader drawn to God in prayer because only He could save the people of our region. Within a short amount of time, we started prayer meetings all over our little church. I think we had up to six of them weekly. God was purifying us and drawing us near Himself. Prayer preceded our witness and

PRAYER PRECEDED OUR WITNESS AND SUSTAINED IT.

sustained it. As time went on, I was a more peaceful young pastor and more content with whatever success God gave us. More were saved, though never to the degree of the first church. But numbers didn't matter as much to me. A few other churches started in our area, and a couple of them grew really fast, reaching many people for Jesus. I wondered, and still do today, if our church was started in order to be a prayer house for the other churches God had called to reach lost people. Even as I write this chapter, nearly 30 years later, the force of the vision and its meaning grabs me. "This kind can come out only by prayer" (Mark 9:29). That's when prayer and evangelism (witness) became a hyphenated term for me, forever linked. Prayer, saving prayer, is witness—Prayer-Witness.

Scripture teaches us many things about prayer and witness. As Paul mentors his apprentice, Timothy, to lead the Ephesian church, he gives him strategic priorities. The first of the priorities is prayer that immerses every aspect of the ministry and especially the witness dimension. Let's take a look.

> *I urge, then, first of all, that petitions, prayers, intercession and thanksgiving be made for all people—for kings and all those in authority, that we may live peaceful and quiet lives in all godliness and holiness. This is good, and pleases God our Savior, who wants all people to be saved and to come to a knowledge of the truth. For there is one God and one mediator between God and mankind, the man Christ Jesus, who gave himself as a ransom for all people. This has now been witnessed to at the proper time.*
>
> —1 Timothy 2:1–6

The force of this prayer directive from Paul to Timothy is found in the first phrase, "I urge, then, first of all." This is not one of many things Timothy must do. It is the *first* thing. First things are at the top of the to-do list. When I'm leading and administrating my work rightly, I prioritize what matters most in a day and do it as close to first as possible. If I have a hard call to make or a confrontation that needs to occur, it is best to do it immediately because my mind is thinking about it all the time anyway. Why? Because it is a first thing.

Prayer is not only a first thing, it is an urgent thing. Paul's first two words are, "I urge." Before we read more than six words in this text, we know we have an urgent first priority, and it's about to be revealed.

Tomorrow is my wedding anniversary. For the 37th time I get to thank God and celebrate His goodness for Marie and being with Marie. Jamieson's Restaurant is our favorite setting for this time. Guess what an urgent first priority is? To make the reservation! It is urgent. Paul's insistence that prayer is urgent means that there is a potential crisis at hand. Just as not getting our reservation at our favorite anniversary restaurant would've been a crisis, or at least would leave me with egg on my face, so too not prioritizing prayer is a potential crisis. We will soon see what that crisis is.

So we've got two things going on here regarding prayer. It is an essential thing, and it is an urgent thing. What is so important and urgent that Paul calls for prayer from his young protégé with such intensity? I argue that the "what" he was to pray about is why it is so essential and urgent. In this passage, the "what" is the salvation of lost people. Here's why.

After the initial call to urgent prayer as a first thing, Paul defines the comprehensive nature of the prayer with four different words, including prayers for ourselves (petitions), prayers for others (intercessions), and prayers of thanksgiving. All these prayers, which I term "comprehensive" praying, are to be made on behalf of "all people" (v. 1). Hold onto the "all people" focus of the prayers for a moment. The "all people" includes kings and government leaders (v. 2) but not exclusively so. Verses 3–4 convey why "all people"—and not just kings and government leaders—are to be prayed for: because "God our Savior . . . wants *all people* to be saved and . . . come to a knowledge of the truth" (author's emphasis). This is the crux of the passage.

The supreme purpose for the comprehensive praying is because God wants all people to be saved and know the truth of Christ. Paul then proceeds to give what I consider the most stunning and eloquent definitions of the gospel of Christ Jesus we find anywhere in the New Testament (vv. 5–6). The apostle is focused like a laser beam on the saving of lost people. Paul knows that comprehensive, aggressive praying is required for that to occur.

You see this focus and his passion for prayer and witness in a brief but poignant autobiographical insertion in Romans 10:1. In this context, Paul is lamenting and longing for the salvation of his people, the Jews. We overlook this sometimes. Because Paul is the supreme witness to the Gentiles, we can miss his longing for his own ethnic group, the Jews. Yet in this passage his heart leaps into his writing, "Brothers and sisters, my heart's desire and prayer to God for the Israelites is that they may be saved." Read how Eugene Peterson expresses this in *The Message*, "Believe me, friends, all I want for Israel is what's best for

Israel: salvation, nothing less. I want it with all my heart and pray to God for it all the time." Paul longs for their salvation, and his theology demands that the longing be acted out in his prayers. Can it be any less for you and me?

A couple of minutes ago, as I was writing this section of the book, I had to stop. I was compelled to pause because the Lord brought to my mind my neighbors and friends who need so very desperately to know Him. I am awestruck by the need and almost teary once again. "Oh, please, my Lord, save them, every one of them. Their life stories, their needs, real and subconscious, their eternal destination are all dependent on them knowing you, my Lord. Please."

It might be surprising, but Jesus is also an advocate on the topic of prayer and its link to salvation. In the Lord's Prayer, He tells us to pray that God's kingdom will come. The kingdom is God's reign over all that is and within all who exist. Sometimes when I pray that perfect prayer, I imagine the words "your kingdom come, your will be done, on earth" (Matthew 6:10) mean making everything that's wrong in the world and in humans restored to a pre-sin state. That certainly includes the souls of lost people. The promise of our Lord someday bringing His kingdom reign gives us hope to hang on and fulfill His calling for our generation.

THE PROMISE OF OUR LORD SOMEDAY BRINGING HIS KINGDOM REIGN GIVES US HOPE TO HANG ON AND FULFILL HIS CALLING FOR OUR GENERATION.

Hebrews 7:24–25 tells us more about our Lord Jesus and the doctrines of prayer and salvation. In this passage our Lord is not teaching about the idea, He is embodying it. "But because Jesus lives forever, his priesthood lasts forever. Therefore he is able, once and forever, to save [completely] those who come to God through him. He lives forever to intercede with God on their behalf" (NLT).

As I understand this, we rejoice that Jesus' work on the Cross saves *completely*. But there is more—and this is mysterious—His ongoing work is intercession: praying while seated at the right hand of the Father. It really is a mystery to me, and I wonder why. But it appears our Lord's prayers participate in the completion of the work of the Cross accomplished in the past.

The older I get the more I see mysteries in the Word as our God reveals His truths. This idea is certainly one of them. But, I also give less attention to trying to discern the whys of those mysteries. I want to understand the whats so that I can be obedient. If Jesus prays for the salvation of humanity, shouldn't we? Makes sense to me. If we accept that this idea of prayer contributing to salvation is correct, how do we enter into its practice? Can it become a holy habit in our lives? Yes, it can. Should it? Absolutely.

I didn't know how to do it, but I knew my little church surely needed it. We were dealing with hardened soil, and only the water of intercession would break it down. I was on a mission to learn about prayer and witness. That is when God began teaching me through two great organizations.

In the fall of 1991, I had my first opportunity to meet Dr. Billy Graham. I was with 12 other younger ministry leaders being mentored by Dr. Graham's son-in-law, Dr. Leighton Ford. Leighton orchestrated a private dinner with Dr. Graham and our group. He told us that Mr. Graham (he preferred the term *Mr.* to *Dr.*, feeling he'd never earned a doctorate and shouldn't be called a doctor, regardless of the honorary award given to him many times) had the time to answer one question from each of us. I believe our discussion time with him following the dinner was limited to about an hour. I went first. I asked a loaded question because I'd read his views on the matter I wanted to discuss and knew of his passion about the issue. The question was, "Do you believe there is a link between prayer and evangelistic impact?" He was directly across from me in a small boardroom. I remember he leaned in, looked at us, and began by saying an emphatic yes.

Mr. Graham talked on the issue for nearly 40 minutes. I remember a few of his points. He said that the only qualitative difference between crusades he'd conducted prior to the historic event of Los Angeles (LA) in 1949 and after was the emphasis on prayer.

See, before he and his team descended on LA in 1949, they called for an informal prayer saturation of the event. Mr. Graham told us that many people traveled to LA on their own to do nothing else but intercede for the planned three-week campaign. He wasn't well known then, so the intercessors were probably friends and acquaintances from other events. The rest is, as they say, history.

The three-week crusade was extended to eight weeks as thousands upon thousands attended the large tent in LA. The *Los Angeles Times* reported 3,000 nonbelievers committed their lives to Christ. They came from every walk of life, from movie stars to gangsters. Even the great newspaper magnate, William

Randolph Hearst, is believed to have attended based on the fact that he telegrammed his newspapers throughout the country with two famous words, "Puff [i.e., promote] Graham."

A former Olympic athlete-turned-prisoner of war in a Japanese camp, Louis Zamperini, also came and gave his life to Christ there. Zamperini's story became the best-selling book and highly acclaimed movie, *Unbroken*.

A lesser-known attendee was a widow named Pearl Goode who was moved to become a prayer warrior for the crusades. Without anyone on the Billy Graham Evangelical Crusade team knowing, she would pay her own way to wherever they were holding an event, check into a hotel, and pray without ceasing. According to an article by Will Graham, Billy Graham's grandson, Pearl estimated she traveled 48,000 miles by bus simply to pray for the crusades.

The world changed overnight for Mr. Graham, and what's more is evangelicalism was becoming a fast-growing movement worldwide.

As we sat at the roundtable discussion, listening to Mr. Graham's description of how prayer boosted the impact of his crusades, he also said there had been times when he postponed or canceled crusades in cities if he sensed the intercessory work was lacking. Yes, he saw an inseparable link between prayer and evangelism impact.

Dr. Bill Bright of Campus Crusade for Christ (now called Cru) believed the same. I remember him saying, "Before you talk to a person about God, talk to God about that person." There is efficacy and practical wisdom in that statement. Through my experience, the Billy Graham Evangelistic Association and Cru are two of the most effective and focused evangelizing organizations of the late twentieth and early twenty-first centuries. The "two Bills" believed in prayer and witness. They practiced it and made it core to their organizations. We can too. We must. I don't think I'm being too dramatic to say that lives depend on it.

So it was my vision of the dirt clod that led me to explore the scriptural and practical association between prayer and evangelism in the local church. It was the "Bills" and their strategic implementation of it that led my staff and me to employ it in our church at about the same time.

Little did I know that by sheer grace this implementation would then help strategically place prayer-evangelism in my denomination in the 1990s. The denomination, the Evangelical Covenant Church, was and is my denominational family. At the time our leaders were lamenting the lack of conversion growth in our churches across America. Soon after, Marie and I were asked to move from our local church to the national offices to energize evangelism for more than 600 churches. We began working with the staff and the board of directors, realizing we had a problem but not sure what to do about it. I was convinced prayer was a key but didn't know what it would look like to employ it across hundreds of churches.

IT WAS THE EVANGELISM PRAYER LIST. EVERY BELIEVER WOULD BE ASKED TO WRITE DOWN THE NAMES OF PEOPLE THEY KNEW WHO WERE FAR FROM GOD AND PROMISE TO PRAY REGULARLY FOR THEM TO COME TO CHRIST.

Then God gave us a breakthrough. One of our most gifted pastors told the evangelism board that parachurch organizations used a strategy of prayer to stimulate witness. He suggested we try it. It was simple, concrete, and easily implemented. It was the evangelism prayer list. Every believer would be asked to write down the names of people they knew who were far from God and promise to pray regularly for them to come to Christ. We gave it a national title, developed an easy-to-reproduce template and logo, and we were up and running.

We called the project Bringing My World to Christ and distributed more than 100,000 pamphlets on the project to the churches. Articles about the power of prayer in witness were dispersed in the national magazine. We literally told people they didn't have to open their mouths in verbal witness until they'd bathed the process and the people they listed in prayer. It caught on like wildfire. One of the best decisions we made was to promise ourselves to keep doing the program for ten years. Why? Because it is easy to keep coming up with new ideas before the better, older ideas have lodged into the lifestyles of believers.

We kept track of the number of people we were praying for and the number of people who made a decision for Christ in the course of a year. Early in the year, local churches started holding Bringing My World to Christ Sundays. People brought a copy of their lists forward, placed them in baskets, and had the pastor(s) consecrate them before God by offering a dedicatory prayer. At the end of each year, the churches would record the number of faith decisions and celebrate God's saving grace. We consecrated names, prayed, and celebrated God's harvest. Here are a few of the numbers we recorded.

In 1991, 200 churches made prayer lists and together prayed for 27,000 people to find Jesus. Ten years later in 2001, 326 churches participated and prayed for 250,000 people. In 1991, we recorded one spiritual decision for every 39 church attendees. By 1995, we recorded an average of one spiritual decision for every 14 attendees. Both the numbers of people being prayed for and the numbers of people making decisions for Jesus grew exponentially. I am not saying the infusion of Prayer-Witness was the only variable influencing this growth, but none of us who were a part of that decade would argue that it played a major role.

Numbers are one thing, but living, breathing stories are quite another. Let me share a story from that era that is forever imprinted on my mind. A youth pastor in Santa Barbara, California, heard about Bringing My World to Christ and sought to employ it with his high school group. As I recall, when he started promoting the upcoming winter retreat, he encouraged his youth to specifically invite their unchurched and lost friends. But he said, "Don't invite them yet. Let's start praying for those we want to invite to be open to accepting our invitation." He encouraged his youth to create a top-ten list. This list would be comprised of the ten kids on campus who were least likely to ever come to a Christian retreat and even less likely to be saved. The youth group was not only going to invite unchurched kids to come, but the kids least likely to come. Once they made their list, they covenanted to pray for each one on the list for weeks before extending the invitations.

Extending the invitations was the tipping-point moment. Would the youth group really invite the kids on the list? It is so hard to actually open our mouths about God. Fear kicks in.

Chances are the youth group kids weren't even close friends with those on the list. It would be very hard to ask them to come. But ask them, they did. Nine of the ten kids on the list said yes and came on the retreat, and eight of them gave their lives to Christ. It was a powerful time in all these kids' lives. God did something great in and through them.

Just in case you need more encouragement to make Prayer-Witness a life practice, I want to share another story. One of our church members, Greg Cox, recently reminded me of a message I preached just a few years ago when I first challenged the congregation to begin practicing Prayer-Witness. We included a prayer card in the bulletin and gave the congregation a few moments to pray and then list the names of anyone who came to mind. The qualification was that these would be people they knew who needed to meet Christ or return to Christ. Greg told me that I also said to list people that seemed nearly impossible to reach. He took that challenge seriously and put five "doozies" (his words, not mine) on his list. Greg did more than pray. The more he prayed, the more he felt drawn to care for and share with the people on his list as God gave opportunity.

Within two years, two of his people had come to faith.

The third person's journey bears repeating. Greg had been asked and agreed to pray for the salvation of his co-worker's spouse. They were experiencing marital troubles as well. One morning while in our worship service, Greg was especially drawn to pray for this situation. Neither the co-worker nor spouse attended our church, so that wasn't the impetus. He simply had an intuitive need to pray. To Greg, this was clearly a word from God. The next morning the co-worker bounded into his office.

"Guess what happened yesterday morning, Greg?"

"May I guess?" Greg asked.

"Yes."

"Your husband came to Christ yesterday?"

Sure enough, that is what occurred. And, in fact, the man's public conversion happened in another church at about the same time Greg was drawn to pray for the man in our church. The fourth and fifth conversions on Greg's doozies list occurred even more recently.

Greg's list included mostly co-workers. One of them left his company, but Greg continued praying for and kept in touch with the person. This person told Greg he could never become a Christian because his wife was an atheist and it would cause a rift in their marriage if he became a Christian. I think the man used the phrase, "She would throw me out." But before long, the man called Greg to tell him he'd become a Christ follower. Even more, his wife, the atheist, had as well!

Such stories leave me awestruck and filled with hope. The youth group in Santa Barbara saw nine people saved within six months. Greg witnessed five persons saved within a few years. It doesn't always occur that fast. It might be more accurate to say it usually takes longer.

Even as I prepared to write this chapter, a distant cousin called me from another state. Forty years ago, two friends and I had evidently shared Christ with her while we were on a motorcycle tour as college students and visited her and my aunt and uncle on their farm in Montana. In recent years we've had more contact as our parents and aunts and uncles age and pass away. Yet, God was at work. I had not prayed continually for her over the last 40 years, but I had prayed for her and most of my distant relatives occasionally. She called to tell me she had fully surrendered her life to Jesus Christ, and she thanked me for my prayers and words about Jesus over the years. A few months, a few years, several decades—the mystery of salvation and our role as witnesses through Prayer and Care and Share is God's work in His time.

What else do we learn from these memorable stories? First and foremost they exemplify the inseparable link between prayer and effective witness. Praying for people to find Christ supernaturally draws them toward God. As we discussed earlier, I don't know why God ordained our prayers to contribute in God's saving mission, but they do. Praying for lost people also draws us to play a role in loving and reaching them. I'm convinced the youth group kids had the gumption and will to invite the kids on their top-ten list because they'd been praying for them. Greg's prayers led him to share as God opened opportunities. As we pray for lost people, God works a miracle in us as He works the miracle in those we pray for. We start loving them as they start looking for and loving God. They move toward God and we move toward them.

Do you have a top-ten list? If you are like me, I have the good problem of my list growing to 20 and 30 and more every year. How do I pray for them all? As I go through my list each week, sometimes I simply offer the names to God. Quite often the Holy Spirit has me linger on one or more names, offering me insight and calling me to pray more for them in their situation. Praying for them once a week leads to praying for some of them more often as well. Just driving past the home of someone on my list leads me to offer them to God for salvation. Other times I wake in the night with one or more people on my heart. When that happens to you, offer them to God. I also encourage readers to use the Scriptures as they pray for people. Often we don't know what to pray, but when we use God's Word, we know and have confidence that we are praying according to God's will. Here are a few Scriptures and their accompanying ideas that may be of help to you:

SCRIPTURES AND PRAYER-WITNESS

1. Pray that God will draw them to Christ. (John 6:44, my favorite)

2. Ask that they will seek to know God. (Matthew 7:7–8)

3. Pray that they will hear and believe God's Word. (Romans 10:17)

4. Ask that they will be delivered from Satan's attempt to blind them to the truth. (2 Corinthians 4:4)

5. Pray that God will send other believers to witness to them. (Matthew 9:38)

6. Pray that they will be convinced that Jesus is Lord and risen from the dead. (Romans 10:9)

7. Pray that they will turn from their sin. (Acts 3:19)

We must not only pray for people far from God but also for our Christian friends and ourselves. Jesus made it clear that people are more ready to find God than Christians are ready to share God with them. "The harvest is plentiful but the workers are few" (Matthew 9:37). That is why Christians need to pray for one another in organic witness living. One of the easiest ways to do this is to simply tell the Lord regularly that we are reporting for witness duty and available for any assignments He has in mind.

Recently I met with a local high school principal. I was not meeting to share Jesus with him, but I was ready should spiritual things pop up in the conversation because I'd reported for witness duty that day. The meeting went very well regarding our agenda, but God also gave an opportunity for a brief interaction of spiritual things. The door opened naturally as he told me about his school and the more than 2,000 youth he sought to educate as principal. That led me to convey that as a pastor he could count on me and our church to be praying for him and his faculty in their important efforts. He expressed thanks, and from there it seemed very natural to simply ask him if he and his family were involved in a church or any kind of spiritual practices. He gave a brief yes and told us about a local church they visit. Another Christian colleague in the meeting then asked him what church it was and a bit more about it. We could perceive that spiritual matters had some, but not deep, importance to him. The discussion didn't go long, but it went well. We planted seeds of gospel witness and invited him and his family to visit our new church in his area if it was ever of interest to him. He responded with gratitude and even asked if he could talk about the high school and its needs at the church if he visited. Of course he could!

Again, the opportunities to share a little or a lot are all around us. Taking a moment each day to tell the Lord we are available for witness has an almost miraculous way of resulting in witness moments.

There are at least four other ways to pray for ourselves and other brothers and sisters as we live out the Witness-Life. A couple of months ago, I had lunch with a good friend and pastor-colleague. We are close enough that we've talked about people we long to see come to know Jesus. We check in with each other as a way of providing caring accountability in the matter. So, it was quite natural for me to ask about his mom, who is still far from God. He was sad about her lack of interest in spiritual things. Even worse, there are times when she is downright antagonistic. He worries about her, of course—what son doesn't—and especially about her life after this life on earth. He then went on to tell me of two opportunities he would have to spend time with her during the upcoming Christmas season. I promised him I would pray for him and her. But how? How do we pray when we promise we will pray for one another's witness opportunities? The Apostle Paul helps us in this area of witness-praying. He teaches about it in his letters to the Ephesians and the Colossians and models three ideas:

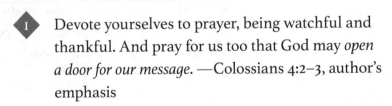

1   Devote yourselves to prayer, being watchful and thankful. And pray for us too that God may *open a door for our message.* —Colossians 4:2–3, author's emphasis

2   Pray also for me, that whenever I speak, *words may be given me.* —Ephesians 6:19, author's emphasis

Pray also for me ... *that I will fearlessly* make known the mystery of the gospel ... Pray *that I may declare it fearlessly*, as I should. —Ephesians 6:19–20, author's emphasis

Note how, in each passage, Paul seeks prayer as he engages in his Witness-Life. Evidently his experience, his intellect, and his training had not convinced him that he didn't need God's help in every witness situation—he knew he did. He asks for three specific things: open doors, the right words, and courage.

OPEN DOORS

Paul relied on God to prepare the situations he entered. Since God goes ahead in every witness venture, Paul trusted that God would prepare the situation as well as the minds and hearts of his listeners. And I think Paul probably counted on God to show him the doors. I know I certainly need that. My busyness combined with my propensity to live in the "next thing" rather than the present moment bothers me a lot. I need God to enable me to live in the "now thing" and see

> I NEED GOD TO ENABLE ME TO LIVE IN THE "NOW THING" AND SEE AND HEAR HIM WITH EXPECTANCY.

and hear Him with expectancy. Sometimes I walk right into doors of spiritual opportunity without even knowing they are witness doors!

One of our pastors once spoke with a young woman who was considering Christ. He asked if she had a Bible. She said she did but was afraid to open it. When he asked why, she confided that she was afraid it would tell her how bad she was, and she already felt bad enough about herself. He responded that the Bible would tell her how bad she was but that even more, it would tell her how good God is and how much He loves her. I believe she gave her life to Christ that day or very soon after.

That was an open door. A door is whenever we see, hear, or sense there is receptivity to spiritual things. You can usually tell if someone is receptive. The questions you ask bring answers that suggest open dialogue is welcome. You can also tell when the listener is not open. We'll talk more about that later, but suffice it to say you can usually tell. Paul prayed for open doors into the hearts and minds of the people he engaged. And he was praying he would see the doors. Help us, Lord!

RIGHT WORDS

Paul also sought God's voice to be his voice. He didn't trust his own thoughts and speech—he sought God's. In 1 Peter 4:11 it says, "If anyone speaks, they should do so as one who speaks the very words of God." Let's be honest, it's not always possible to know when I'm speaking my thoughts or God's thoughts. But prayer for God's voice to govern one's own is a vital practice. Evidently it is something so important to Paul that he seeks prayer for it. I've had hundreds of experiences when I've responded to questions or statements with ideas and words that I didn't know I had in me. This happens a lot in preaching. Pastors often go off script as they sense God moving them to elaborate or express an idea differently from what was originally recorded in their notes or manuscript.

PRAYER FOR GOD'S VOICE TO GOVERN ONE'S OWN IS A VITAL PRACTICE.

This happened to me not long ago while riding to the airport in a taxi. I was writing in the backseat and engaging in very little conversation with the driver. At one point I had the notion (God-nudge) to quit writing about Witness-Life and see if there was an open door for spiritual conversation. So, I put my writing away and asked God for guidance.

Conversation ensued, and a door opened to ask a spiritual question. It didn't open up until the last ten minutes of the ride, but then the door opened widely. God gave me the right questions to ask the driver, leading her to share about her desire to get closer to God. The conversation ended with me giving her a small booklet about faith in Christ and inviting her to visit my church and ask for me.

IT IS SO WONDERFUL TO HAVE GOD WITH US TO WAKE US UP AND SEE THAT THE HARVEST IS READY FOR WITNESS.

Even as I review that moment, I am stunned by the way the conversation moved and the clear path the Lord provided. Now, I have to admit there were a couple of pregnant pauses when I wondered if anything spiritual would transpire. Sometimes there is nothing. But on that day there was. God opened a door and gave me His words, and I'm laughing at myself and thanking God for the nudge. Oh, it is so wonderful to have God with us to wake us up and see that the harvest is ready for witness. Praise to Him.

COURAGE

Take a moment to look back at Ephesians 6:19–20. Paul asks for prayer that he will be fearless. Then he repeats himself and asks for it a second time. It seems to me this was the preeminent issue on his mind. If he asks and then asks again for prayer to be fearless in his Witness-Life, it must mean he struggled with fear I've seldom met a Christian who does not experience fear in witnessing. We will talk about fear more fully toward the end of the book. The point here is that Paul knew he needed prayer to beat back the temptation to not witness because of fear. I emphasize the word *temptation* because once I realized I was being tempted by the evil one not to witness, I began to deal with it like any other temptation. God promises the way to escape temptation (I Corinthians 10:13). Like Paul, like us. "Lord, deliver us from the temptation to fall to paralyzing fear in our Witness-Life. Give us courage to open our mouths."

This notion of how to pray for ourselves and other believers in Witness-Life is crucial to our impact, and—at least in my life and the world of believers I walk with—too little employed. If all the forces of hell are organized to keep people from the saving life of Jesus Christ, then we must be sober-minded and remember, "This kind only comes out by prayer" (Mark 9:29). To sum it up then, pray for open doors, effective words, and courage to speak.

CHAPTER 6

Care-Witness

I DIDN'T grow up in a religious home. I visited a church one time, on Easter when I was in the fifth grade, and thought it was the strangest place I'd ever seen. Mom and Dad just didn't think it was important to get into religion, though they never spoke badly about it as far as I remember. After becoming a Christian in my late teens, I started attending a local evangelical church of about 350 people. They were friendly and welcoming of teens finding Jesus in the Jesus Movement. I was one of them.

The Jesus Movement was occurring in the United States at the same time as the countercultural movements of the 60s and 70s, which would impact the emerging generation that would soon be known as baby boomers. I grew up 20 miles from Berkley, California, a place of civil rights and war protests. It was also known for promoting sexual freedom, recreational drugs, and a lot more. Those themes and choices spread throughout the country. Some of it was positive; most of it has brought increased promiscuity, lack of direction, and misery.

But, God was also on the move, especially in cities of our nation near universities and colleges. Kids started turning to Jesus as the countercultural movement's promises failed. Parachurch ministries, especially those focused on the evangelization of young baby boomers, flourished. Many churches, especially those willing to offer the gospel with more contemporary forms of music and the arts, also thrived. I was saved in that era and began reaching other youth for Christ immediately. I planted churches for unchurched and underchurched people. Large numbers were converted.

I'm sure I invited my parents to try out Jesus and come to my local church. I don't think they did, though, at least not until I got very sick when I was 20 years old and was rushed the hospital with internal bleeding. That would start to change a lot of things about God and life in our family. I lost a lot of blood while the doctors were, for two weeks, mystified as to the source of my troubles. I remember being told that over half the blood in my body was lost. Therefore, I needed a lot of blood to replace it. I would lose blood almost as fast as they could put it in me. My parents looked for help at a blood bank, but it was very expensive. Our family health insurance would cover some of the costs, but it was still taxing on my middle-class parents.

The church was praying for me as an update regarding my condition was sent out to prayer circles. The pastors and some of the kids in the youth group visited me, and Mom and Dad, who visited every day, got to meet some of the church people for the first time. My parents felt the church's love for me and were grateful for the prayers. It was the church on display with the love of Christ, and it was impressive to behold.

Finally, the doctors did exploratory surgery and discovered an intestinal ulcer. They were able to stop the bleeding through surgery. I would have to stay in the hospital another week to make sure the blood loss ceased and to receive enough blood to restore me. My parents didn't care how much it would cost to get their son well, but it was going to put a dent in their small savings.

Unbeknownst to me, the church was doing more than visiting and praying. They were also giving funds to help with my medical costs. Toward the end of my stay in the hospital, we heard that one of the men in our church who worked in corporate America had been able to utilize a blood bank account they had for their employees and completely cover all the costs of my blood. They donated from their reserves for me, a total stranger.

The love of the church and its people—their time, their prayers, their tangible expressions of love such as cards and flowers, and the giving of blood—overwhelmed my parents. When I was able to go back to church, Mom and Dad decided to start coming too. They didn't know how to sing a hymn or find the Scripture preached in the pew Bibles, but they wanted to thank the church that had cared for their son. Through this ministry, they found the love that had been poured out on their son, also freely given to them.

Over time, Mom started going to a women's Bible study and discovered, or rediscovered, the faith of her childhood. My parents sat about two-thirds of the way back on the right side of the church on Sundays. A couple of years after I became the youth director of the church, I was asked to preach one Sunday. I don't remember the text or how well I did. It couldn't have been very good because I was young and just starting my ministry. But I know I must have spoken about the One who had "donated" His blood for us all and how our sins were forgiven because of His sacrifice. I know I must've done that because at the end of the message, I gave an invitation for people to believe in and receive Jesus as Lord. Two-thirds of the way back on the right side near the aisle next to the stained-glass windows, I saw my father raise his hand to say yes to God, starting him on a many years' journey toward loving God.

THE LOVE OF CHRIST IN GOD'S PEOPLE ADORNED THE GOSPEL WORDS ABOUT HIM.

The gospel was displayed by God's church, the body of Christ, to my parents. It opened their minds and hearts to the person of Christ. The love of Christ in God's people adorned the gospel words about Him. Eternity now houses Jim and Peggy Allison, who are waiting to reunite with their children again.

The work of the church in the lives of my parents is a beautiful testimony of Care-Witness. You may have a similar story as well. Most believers respond readily and happily to the call to adorn the gospel with loving works. The word *adorn*, however, may be new to you as you think about Care-Witness. To adorn something is to dress it up or clothe it as in the case of one's wardrobe or to describe decorating something like a Christmas tree.

When I was in my thirties, I had two part-time jobs. In addition to working as a pastor, I was also a professional actor in the San Francisco Bay Area. I did both those jobs for about seven years. Neither paid very well, but I liked them both very much. And, not surprisingly, reaching people for Jesus happened in both jobs. The acting work gave me deepening insights into the beauty and the sorrows of life and gave me more love and understanding for the lost. But to be honest, there was one part of being a professional actor I didn't like.

An actor has to be both a skilled artist of the soul and a salesman! I loved the first part of that and hated the second. I had to constantly market myself—*yuck*. Auditions for roles in commercials, television shows, plays, or films required competing constantly for every part. An audition would often gather 10–50 skilled professional actors who looked a lot like each other. How could an actor possibly stand out enough to land the job? Most of the time I didn't. In the big markets of New York and Los Angeles, if an actor lands 10 percent of the roles he auditions for, he is considered very successful. In places like San Francisco, the success rate grows to 20 percent of auditions. We failed most of the time.

One of the ways to stand out, however, among a highly trained and skilled set of actors was through wardrobe. (I bet you wondered if this story would ever get around to the adorn idea.) What I wore, or how I adorned myself, prior to the audition could help me get the part. An actor that dressed for the part was smart and had a leg up. But the really, really smart ones also chose their most flattering colors to accentuate their wardrobe. Clothing and the colors of the clothing adorn the actor, giving him or her the best chance to win the part.

Colors? Yes! That's because God, in His perfect and unique creation of humans, gave each of us hues of skin and hair color that accentuate us individually. The colorists who help discern your colors usually place your palette within a season. For instance, I am a spring with fall overtones. So, am I saying a wardrobe and the right colors would land the job? Was that enough? No, of course not. Performance matters most. But adornment in clothing and coloring certainly helps. Paul's use of the term "adorn" in Titus 2:10 (ESV) has this meaning. But instead of wardrobe or decorations adorning someone or something, our good works adorn or accentuate gospel words. Using the language of this book then, Care-Witness adorns Share-Witness.

In Titus 2, Paul instructs three groups of people whose actions as believers adorn the Christian message positively or negatively. He first calls for older women in the faith to live godly lives around younger women and guide them in how to likewise live godly lives (vv. 3–5). Why? Paul says, "so that no one will malign the word of God" (v. 5). Secondly, he instructs young men to live godly and self-controlled lives (vv. 6–8). Why? He says, "so that those who oppose you [nonbelievers] may be ashamed because they have nothing bad to say about us" (v. 8). Finally, Paul addresses slaves, or family servants (vv. 9–10). Paul asks them to serve respectfully and be trustworthy in every way "so that in everything they may *adorn* the doctrine of God our Savior" (ESV, author's emphasis).

In each of these cases, the deep purpose of living holy and noble lives is not to receive more blessings from God but rather to be a blessing of God to a lost world. Our Spirit-led character lived in the open—in our homes, neighborhoods, and workplaces—adorns and gives credence to the doctrine of salvation.

> THE DEEP PURPOSE OF LIVING HOLY AND NOBLE LIVES IS NOT TO RECEIVE MORE BLESSINGS FROM GOD BUT RATHER TO BE A BLESSING OF GOD TO A LOST WORLD.

Paul concludes the thought in verse 11, which moves me every time I read it, "For the grace of God has appeared that offers salvation to all people." The weight of this truth is daunting. My behavior in the world mysteriously participates in the communication of the gospel, offering God's grace to the world.

Therefore, the first arena of our Care-Witness is to live Spirit-filled lives adorned with the character of God around all people. Personally, I immediately realize I'm not a very good witness in this sense because I'm so loaded with sinful tendencies. If God's gospel is dependent on my lifestyle, God's got a problem. Yet, another part of me knows that God is expert at using broken vessels for His glory. Every character in the Bible, except for Jesus, is evidence of that. God is determined to continually make us more like His Son. That gives me hope. Yep, God is making us better every day and in every way as we yield our lives to Him.

The great theologian (*not*), Paul McCartney of The Beatles, wrote about this in a song, "I've got to admit it's getting better. It's a little better all the time (it can't get no worse)." There is some truth to that. I've been taught by mentors far wiser than myself that the display of Christian character, which adorns the words of the gospel, is as evident by how quickly we repent and ask forgiveness when we are at our worst as it is when we are adorned with the Spirit's goodness. I think this means that our humility is as compelling as holiness to those far from God.

THE DISPLAY OF CHRISTIAN CHARACTER, WHICH ADORNS THE WORDS OF THE GOSPEL, IS AS EVIDENT BY HOW QUICKLY WE REPENT AND ASK FORGIVENESS WHEN WE ARE AT OUR WORST AS IT IS WHEN WE ARE ADORNED WITH THE SPIRIT'S GOODNESS.

Care-Witness starts with our character and then naturally moves out through our actions. Author and pastor John Maxwell said in his book *Winning with People*, "People don't care how much you know until they know how much you care." Peter wrote, "Live such good lives among the pagans [Gentiles, ESV] that, though they accuse you of doing wrong, they may see your good deeds and glorify God on the day he visits us" (1 Peter 2:12). Good deeds witness of God's glory and attributes to the world. The words of the gospel can be denied or pressed against by those we long to see know Christ, but good works are hard to dismiss. Even Jesus speaks of this. "Do not believe me unless I do the works of my Father. But if I do them, even though you do not believe me, believe the works, that you may know and understand that the Father is in me, and I in the Father" (John 10:37–38). As I think back on the story of my illness and how God's people did good deeds in such a way that my parents saw something radically different about Christians, I see what both Peter and our Lord described.

The obvious question is how do we make good deeds—or Care-Witness—part of our lifestyle. First of all, we know that most people trace their journey to God through people they know. I hope you took the time to remember and record the names of people who helped you come to or come back to Jesus Christ. We will have the most impact on people who know us. That's not to say occasional interactions with strangers or near-strangers don't play a part. They do. But, by and large, your life and deeds play best with people you know. Please take about 30 seconds to look at the following chart. I call it the "Circle of Nearness," and it portrays this truth quite well. I didn't come up with the term and honestly can't remember who did, but it is very helpful.

CARE—LOVE BEYOND THE EXPECTED

YOUR CIRCLE OF NEARNESS

- FRAN-gelism
  Effective
  Long-term
  Exhausting
- STRAN-gelism
  Effective
  Short-term
  Exhilarating

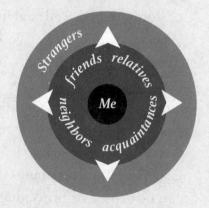

The nearer we are in relationships to people the greater our evangelistic impact both in good works and good words (a.k.a. Care and Share). I've heard this witnessing relationship called "FRAN-gelism." I like the designation. Our relationships are generally in one of the four categories: (F)riends, (R)elatives, (A)cquaintances/associates, and (N)eighbors. This makes perfect sense. Personal faith is an intimate and meaningful part of life. We don't tend to talk about personal and meaningful things with strangers.

Recently, our daughter was due to have our first grandchild. During that time I shared our hopes, joy, and fears with friends and associates. Once while waiting to get our car serviced, my daughter sent a text telling me that her doctor's appointment was all good news and her daughter and our granddaughter was right on schedule. There were at least ten strangers in this room, and reading her text almost made me cry. It was such good news. However, I didn't tell all the people around me. They were strangers, and it was very personal. It's the same with faith. Our words and our works are most valued within existing relationships.

Now, it is true that displaying and sharing our faith with people we know is also harder. As the chart indicates, FRAN-gelism is effective, but it is also long-term and at times exhausting because of the up and down nature of ongoing relationships. God may ask us to care for someone in special ways for many years.

When God places us into the life of a stranger, also known as "STRAN-gelism," it can be effective but is usually short-lived. In such cases God uses us to provide one-time extraordinary care or share, planting a seed that others in relationship with the person will carry to deeper levels. Occasionally, interaction with a stranger is intended to lead a person to a full faith decision. Public evangelists have this responsibility. FRAN-gelism prepares the hearts so evangelists or other STRAN-gelists are able to reap the harvest. STRAN-gelism is exhilarating whenever we are doing Care-Witness. A short-term missions trip restoring the home of a displaced family suffering from a natural disaster is tremendously fulfilling to the strangers doing and receiving the work.

I encourage people to look at their prayer list of people who don't know Jesus and ask God to allow them to provide Care-Witness as well. In this sense, the list prepared for prayer becomes the list for care and, as you will read later, for share. I can imagine the protests. *I have 30 people I'm praying for, and this author is now asking me to provide Care-Witness to them as well? There is no way I have the time for that.* I couldn't agree more. You can pray for many, care for some, and share with a few in the course of a year. This is where the image of a cone is helpful. I first saw this type of diagram from John Maxwell. In it he demonstrates how you can share with many people but only share deeply with a few. I found much wisdom in that approach and adapted it later with the language of Prayer, Care, Share.

CARE—LOVE BEYOND THE EXPECTED

PRAYER *(many)*
Pray frequently.

CARE *(some)*
Talk often.
Do something occasionally.

SHARE *(few)*
Share as
opportunities
arise.

The cone image reminds me to let God lead me to those He wants me to have special care for over a period of time. As I write I'm looking out the window to my neighborhood where Marie and I have so many neighbors who are friends. Only a couple of them know Jesus Christ in a personal and meaningful way. So, we pray for them all. But this year our opportunities to provide *extraordinary* care will be limited to a few. There will be a couple of block parties where we will be with all our neighbors. In fact just an hour ago I met with a believing couple we'll cohost the "welcome to springtime" neighborhood party with. There will be jogs around the block during which I will stop and chat with others. That is just general neighborliness. But one or more of them will need us in special ways.

YOUR PRAYERS FOR PEOPLE WILL HEIGHTEN YOUR SENSITIVITY TO GOD'S LEADING.

One of our neighbors is dying of cancer this year. It came on suddenly and is devastating. He has been searching and asking lots of questions about Jesus and has been for a few years. But now, he needs me more. I need to be there when the grief is most acute. I provide materials, as a pastor, that can help bring comfort. I can hang out with him if he lets me and talk about the Cubs and about cancer. Incidentally, providing lots of care is never a burden really. I really like my neighbor. I love him. I think he likes me too. And, Jesus said it is always more blessed to give than receive (Acts 20:35). To love him and be loved by him as his neighbor is deeply meaningful.

So how do we begin to show extraordinary care? First, your prayers for people will heighten your sensitivity to God's leading. He will guide you to people and give you ideas in how to care. Once you've identified the people God is guiding you to provide extra care to, consider the decisions below to help make your interactions most effective.

TIME

First, you can offer time. Many would likely say time is the most precious commodity in our lives. The Apostle Paul tells us twice to make the most of every opportunity (Ephesians 5:16; Colossians 4:5). The Colossians passage ties in directly to Care- and Share-Witness, and the Ephesians passage can also be read similarly. Time is the key decision. Most of us don't have the time to care for others if we look at it from a worldly point of view. My taxes are due soon, and I haven't started on them. I have a book deadline. You are reading it, so somehow it got done. We are starting a new campus at our church, and I'm in charge of that.

WHEN WE FOCUS ON HIS STUFF, WE CAN COUNT ON GOD TO TAKE CARE OF ALL THE OTHER STUFF OF LIFE, NAMELY MAKING TIME FOR PEOPLE WHO NEED GOD.

My daughter will have a baby any day, and they need to see us. The "service vehicle" light is on in both our cars. My story is your story.

So, how do we make time to care? This is where we lean deeply on God. When Jesus said, "Seek first his kingdom and his righteousness, and all these things will be given to you as well" (Matthew 6:33), He was talking about all the needs of life. Caring for FRANs is kingdom stuff. God so loved the world that He's left us here. When we focus on His stuff, we can count on God to take care of all the other stuff of life, namely making time for people who need God. This is not idealistic writing. This is God's truth.

PRIORITIZE

God may ask you to give something up to give more to Care-Witness. What I am about to write will not sit well with some pastors. You know how I know? Because I'm a pastor, and this doesn't sit well with me! If you are reading this book, you are most likely a devoted Christian, and that means you are probably also attending and serving in numerous church functions every week. Here comes the bomb. It's time to cut back. *There, I said it.* If we are always at church or doing church things, we won't have time for people who are far from God. I often ask groups of highly dedicated Christians who attend our Prayer, Care, Share seminars to tithe their church time to FRANs. If you are serving and attending church five hours a week, consider giving 30 of those minutes to a co-worker, neighbor, or friend. If you are spending ten hours per week at church, consider cutting out an hour and hanging out with a FRAN. Of course, the tithe of church life doesn't have to be measured weekly. Perhaps each month you can do something with someone you love who is far from God.

MULTITASK

Spending time with people you know who don't know Jesus can take place when you are participating in hobbies, practicing fitness, or doing volunteer community work. I have a pastor-friend who takes a yoga class at the local community center. He is the only man in the class! He joined to get in shape and to meet people outside of his church. Over time it has become known that he is a Christian pastor, and many conversations occur before and after class. A man doing yoga is a bit of a stretch (*pun intended*), but God is enabling him to care for his body and care for people outside his church.

One person I know joined a photography club. I know Christian men who restore and race cars. These individuals are doing what they love in a world of people who need God. Many Christians love to serve social needs in their communities. I have heard of Christians setting up space in their yards for a community garden. Others serve in ministry to homeless people, refugee resettlement, and so much more. Charities, service clubs, PTAs, homeschooling networks. There are myriad ways to provide Christ's love in every setting where we are with people who don't yet know Him.

If you'd like to know more about how to serve your community, I encourage you to read my colleague Lynn Cory's book

Neighborhood Initiative and the Love of God. He is part of a network within several American cities promoting Christian love to the neighborhood, communities, and cities. It's very inspiring.

What you do is up to you. Remember: just being with someone you care about is practicing Care-Witness. It doesn't have to be some deep, heavy need. It might just be an opportunity for coffee, a walk, or a casual lunch, and the discussion might not even venture into spiritual topics. Prioritizing the gift of time to be with people is caring.

Remember, too, letting your friends, co-workers, and neighbors care for you is also a gift.

Here are a few examples. Now before you read these you have to remember or look up an old song by Paul Simon called "50 Ways to Leave Your Lover." The melody is the same, but I changed the words to make them about loving people, not leaving them!

50 WAYS TO LOVE YOUR NEIGHBOR

The problem is all inside your heads, God said to me.

The answer is easy if you think it scripturally.

I'd like to help you learn to witness easily.

There must be 50 ways to love your neighbor, 50 ways to love your neighbor.

Say hi from your yard, Gerard.

Visit walking the dog, Claude.

Make cookies to share, Claire.

Set your Witness-Life free.

Hold a summertime party, Marti.

Invite them for the game, James.

Have them over for dinner, Kimmer.

Set your Witness-Life free.

Yes, the problem is all inside our heads, God said to me.

The answer is easy if we think it scripturally.

I'd like to help you learn to witness easily.

There must be 50 ways to love your . . .

I've also reconfigured the lyrics to provide help in the workplace.

50 WAYS TO LOVE CO-WORKERS

The problem is all inside your heads, God said to me.

The answer is easy if you think it scripturally.

I'd like to help you learn to witness easily.

There must be 50 ways to love co-workers, 50 ways to love co-workers.

Bring bagels to work, Burt.

Avoid gossip in the office, Wallace.

Learn co-workers names, Jane.

Set your Witness-Life free.

Give a compliment or two, Sue.

Promise prayers for their needs, Reed.

Always do a great job, Rob.

Set your Witness-Life free.

Yes, the problem is all inside our heads, God said to me.

The answer is easy if we think it scripturally.

I'd like to help you learn to witness easily.

There must be 50 ways to love your . . .

Before I bring this chapter to a close, I want to offer one additional way to deeply love and serve FRANs and strangers that combines Prayer, Care, and Share. Offering prayer for people is a tremendous gift and act of love. James reminds us, "The prayer of a righteous person is powerful and effective" (James 5:16). Peter says the same, "For the eyes of the Lord are on the righteous and his ears are attentive to their prayer" (1 Peter 3:12). You and I may not feel righteous because of our tendency toward sin, but we have been made righteous in God's mind because Jesus took our sin on Himself and imputed His righteousness to us. How wonderful is the grace of God. In our positions as righteous and adopted heirs in God's own family, we have the enormous privilege and responsibility of praying for people, especially people far from God.

When a FRAN shares a need, it is often perfectly appropriate to ask if you can pray for that need before the conversation concludes. If you perceive that it would not be appropriate, then promise continued prayer as you depart from each other.

Recently, a dear neighbor stopped by to drop off a baby gift for our granddaughter. It was an act of love to us. We love these neighbors, and over the years both this neighbor and his wife have occasionally attended our informational coed Bible studies. One has some Christian background but the other very little. As our neighbor was walking back to her car, she turned to me and said, "Please pray for me." The next day Marie called her to thank her for the gift, and again the neighbor asked for prayer. She didn't go into specifics, but she wants our prayers for her personal needs. The reason she asked is because we have often said to these neighbors and others that we pray for them. Sometimes during the dark, winter months, we even place an electric candle in a front window that is a daily reminder we are praying for our neighbors. They love it, and we love doing it.

You can offer prayer for strangers too. Very often when we are at a restaurant preparing to pray over our meal, we ask the server if there is anything we can pray about for him or her. Of the hundreds of times we've done this, only once or twice has a server said no. It's almost always yes. Often it opens doors to further conversation. Praying for people is our greatest way to do Care-Witness and, as I said previously, links together Prayer, Care, and Share.

We must believe God hears these prayers because He says He does. I write this because I forget how much access and authority we've been given by God through prayer. I start to take it for granted. And, to be honest, sometimes I doubt prayer's power because so often it seems prayers are not answered, or at least not in the way I hoped. I believe God is always answering our prayers for healing in the realm of the soul, even if not in healing for the body. I am also beginning to think God sometimes answers the prayers for physical healing and miracles more for those who are far from God than for those who are already His children.

A group of us were in the Holy Land a couple of years ago and met with a couple of missionaries reaching Arab Muslims and those of nominal Christian backgrounds. One missionary was from the United States and the other from Palestine. We'd been told these two brothers often see dramatic results to their prayers. As we met over a long breakfast in a Bethlehem restaurant, we listened to the stories of the numbers of house churches they were starting. We also asked about their prayers for these people. They carefully told us several stories of dramatic answered prayer. At one point in the conversation I asked if they had any idea what percentage of the people they prayed for saw physical healing or miraculous answers to their problems. They looked at each other as if it was a new question and not something they'd given a lot of thought to. They discussed it for a minute and then said it was fair to say that 40–45 percent of the people prayed for saw dramatic answers. We were astounded. They were surprised that we were astounded because it is simply the world they live in. Then they offered more.

The 40–45 percent was only when applied to non-Christians. They agreed that no more than 5 percent of Christians who sought their prayers saw dramatic results. What a paradigm shift. On the surface of it, it made no sense. In fact, prior to this discussion, I would've thought the percentages would be reversed. But as we talked and thought more about it, it started becoming clear. In the Gospels and in Acts the dramatic answers to prayer are called "signs and wonders." The miracles and healings are not ends in themselves. Most often they point to something much more. They point to the reality of a Sovereign God and His power to mend not only bodies but much more—souls. Christians may actually be healed less in their bodies because the greater healing (of the soul) has already occurred. Christians are healed for eternity. Healings, miracles, visions, and dreams more often occur in places where there are very few Christians. God testifies of His eternal rescue of humanity through His temporary rescue of broken bodies and situations on the temporal plane. It's worth thinking about, isn't it? I share these ideas I learned in the Middle East to increase our faith in the power of prayer for people far from God in the Western world.

All the ways of providing Care-Witness mentioned in this chapter have to do with us caring for our FRANs. But there is one more way that has nothing to do with our actions; rather, it has to do with our FRANs' actions. Let them care for you! Friendship is a two-way street. People not only need to be loved, they need to love. In our neighborhood, our friendships have grown and our Witness-Life is more authentic because we've asked for and allowed our neighbors to care for us.

When both my parents died a few years ago, my neighbor across the street came by. He'd lost both his parents as a young man. I was sitting out on our front porch swing when Jerry came over. He said how sorry he was and allowed me to talk about my grief. His listening to my pain was so helpful. He's a contractor by profession. I'm a pastor. But on that day we exchanged roles. We'd been casual friends prior to that day, but since then we've drawn closer. Jerry doesn't have much faith in God. He's seen a lot of hard things in life and wonders if God is good. He may even wonder if God exists. But our relationship has more mutual understanding and trust because friendship both gives and takes. I'm still hoping for some serious talk with Jerry about Jesus. He's not been a part of our men's investigative Bible study yet. When I last invited him, he said he wasn't ready. I keep praying, hoping, and waiting. What I am sure of, however, is that we have a strong trust and appreciation for each other. A big part of that is because I need him as much as he needs me.

Finally, I must offer a cautionary note on the subject of Care-Witness. In the Western church (Europe, North America, and Oceania), there are some who argue for Care-Witness as the end all of witness. They posit that we've had too many gospel words and too many words that were not backed up by good actions broadcast throughout our societies. Often the argument utilizes a legendary statement many attribute to St. Francis of Assisi, but we don't actually know who said it. It goes like this, "Preach the gospel at all times, and if you must, use words." It is a hyperbolic statement arguing for Christians to major on good works much more than good words. It is helpful in the sense that in those places where there is no Care-Witness, gospel words mean little. I can live with that idea. But my experience in the last two decades of the twentieth century and now in the first two of the twenty-first is that Christians are not most in danger of saying words that are too harsh or too many. The greater danger is saying no words at all. We often keep our mouths closed and hope somehow that the receivers of our Care-Witness will mystically realize our goodness and care has its roots in Jesus Christ.

Some things simply must be said. My former colleague and former president at Wheaton College Duane Litfin has written eloquently on the subject of the power of words, both oral and written, and how in the communication process, words are utilized to bring meaning and understanding to ideas. Nonverbal communication has an important place but cannot replace words when only words will do. Duane takes a close look at these precepts in his book *Word versus Deed*. Similarly, Ed Stetzer, a noted missiologist and evangelism leader, often takes the St. Francis misinterpretation and offers this revision to expose the impossibility of the statement: "Feed the poor at all times, and if you must, use food." It is just as unconvincing.

THE GREATER DANGER IS SAYING NO WORDS AT ALL. WE OFTEN KEEP OUR MOUTHS CLOSED AND HOPE SOMEHOW THAT THE RECEIVERS OF OUR CARE-WITNESS WILL MYSTICALLY REALIZE OUR GOODNESS AND CARE HAS ITS ROOTS IN JESUS CHRIST.

I understand the tendency to want to display our witness with good works more than good words. It is easier, and to be honest, we get lots of accolades for doing so. Of course, the truth is if we depend on our good works to be the only gospel people receive, we're doing irreparable harm when our deeds aren't good. No Christian can display goodness all the time. The longer your lost neighbor, co-worker, or relative knows you, the more they'll see there are cracks in your armor. It's far better to let them know as soon as possible that any good in us comes from God's goodness and not our inner goodness, because we aren't inherently good!

Gospel words don't always make people love us. They often alienate us from society. That's because while the gospel presented as the love of God for the world brings rave reviews from people, gospel words of the reality of sin in all humanity and the penalty it occasions do not. There is bad news in the good news, and you can only truly know how great the good news of grace is when you know how bad the bad news is.

Max De Pree, in his book *Leadership Jazz*, tells about when his granddaughter Zoe was born prematurely. Max's daughter was left to raise the baby on her own, as the father was no longer in the picture. Realizing this, a nurse approached Grandpa Max and said, "For the next several months, at least, you are the surrogate father. I want you to come to the hospital every day to visit Zoe, and when you come, I would like you to rub her body and her legs and arms with the tip of your finger. While you're caressing her, you should tell her over and over how much you love her because she has to be able to connect your voice to your touch." Care-Witness is like that. Care and share are the complete love package with people disconnected from Jesus.

IF WE DEPEND ON OUR GOOD WORKS TO BE THE ONLY GOSPEL PEOPLE RECEIVE, WE'RE DOING IRREPARABLE HARM WHEN OUR DEEDS AREN'T GOOD. NO CHRISTIAN CAN DISPLAY GOODNESS ALL THE TIME.

CHAPTER 7

Share-Witness

"IT'S time to jump," yelled the man instructing me to skydive for the first time. He was a professional and my buddy for the jump. That meant he was literally hooked to me as we carefully rolled from a sitting position to our knees and crawled toward the open door of the airplane. We were about to jump out of the plane together. I hadn't been scared up to that point. In fact, I was up for the adventure of skydiving, that is, until we got to the edge of the plane, an inch away from the open door. I looked out to see the ground 14,000 feet below. Suddenly this adventure made no sense at all. Fear gripped me. That's when he yelled, "Jump now!" A big part of me did not want to. But it was a little late to turn back, so I jumped. As you can tell, I'm still alive and well—ready to tell the story. I carry the memory of the free fall and the opening chute. It was the most exhilarating, fun (one minute free-falling), and peaceful (five minutes of floating down beneath the open parachute) time of my life.

PRAYER-WITNESS CAN BE DONE IN SECRET, CARE-WITNESS CAN BE DONE WITHOUT WORDS, BUT SHARE-WITNESS MEANS WE MUST TALK ABOUT OUR LORD. WORDS ARE ESSENTIAL.

Sharing our faith in Jesus Christ, or Share-Witness, is a little bit like skydiving was for me that day. It too contains fear, exhilaration, joy, and peacefulness all wrapped into one. But you have to jump. The fear in the Witness-Life seems to kick in only when we open our mouths and actually talk with people about Jesus. It's different than prayer and care. Prayer-Witness can be done in secret, Care-Witness can be done without words, but Share-Witness means we must talk about our Lord. Words are essential. Paul wrote in Romans 10:13–14 (NLT):

> *"Everyone who calls on the name of the Lord will be saved."*
> *But how can they call on him to save them unless they believe*
> *in him? And how can they believe in him if they have never*
> *heard about him? And how can they hear about him unless*
> *someone tells them?*

God so loved the world that He left us here. We are given the stewardship of the gospel message to the world. What an amazing and daunting privilege.

In one sense we can't help but do it. Paul said, "For when I preach the gospel, I cannot boast, since I am compelled to preach" (1 Corinthians 9:16). It seems something—or better, *Someone*—compelled him to share. As we are filled daily with the Spirit, and He pours out His love for a lost world into us, it will be quite natural and organic to talk about our faith. But it is more than a compulsion. It is a command. Jesus said, "Go into all the world and preach the gospel to all creation" (Mark 16:15). Similarly, in Matthew, Jesus said, "All authority in heaven and on earth has been given to me. Therefore go and make disciples of all nations" (Matthew 28:18–19). He states His authority over all of existence and then says, therefore, do this! The first command from the resurrected Lord of heaven and earth is to go and witness. Wow. We are compelled and we are commanded. That's pretty good motivation if you ask me.

In the following three chapters, I will discuss the three stages of Share-Witness. To keep it simple, I'll refer to them as Share 1, Share 2, and Share 3. Sometimes you may only reach one or two stages of Share-Witness. Other times you'll have the opportunity to share all three over a period of time.

I am currently two days away from a trip to Israel where 12 of us will enter into Arab-Israeli towns asking God for opportunities to witness of Jesus as the Son of God and Lord of our lives. I'm a bit nervous. The majority of people we'll meet are religious-but-not-radical Muslims. We will go in praying and believing God has appointments for us and that His Word will do what He wishes. Recall the wonderful truth from Isaiah 55:10–11:

> *As the rain and the snow come down from heaven, and do not return to it without watering the earth and making it bud and flourish, so that it yields seed for the sower and bread for the eater, so is my word that goes out from my mouth: It will not return to me empty, but will accomplish what I desire and achieve the purpose for which I sent it.*

This gives me great confidence in God, who has said His Word would do the work. We are ready to jump!

CHAPTER 8

Share 1
Their Story

RECENTLY, a colleague and dear friend from church walked into my office more jovial than usual. Why? He'd returned from a two-hour lunch that wasn't supposed to be two hours. It went that long because God designed one of His divine appointments for my colleague Brian. While sitting at a lunch counter at a Mexican restaurant, Brian ordered flan, an especially luscious dessert. When his order arrived, it was huge—too much to eat. So Brian interrupted the stranger sitting next to him at the counter and said, "Dude, this is way too big for me. Would you like some of this?" The man said yes, and thus began a long serendipitous discussion about life and then God. I wish I'd been there just to watch.

One question led to another, and before Brian knew it, he and a stranger were talking about things that matter in life. His story is a beautiful example of how our God places His people in unique and wonderful places to talk with others about Him. We enter their journey for a few moments to plant spiritual seeds or water seeds already there.

Brian's experience at the Mexican restaurant is an example of the first stage of Share-Witness: Share 1. This kind of sharing has more to do with asking questions and listening than it does with talking. James tells us to be quick to listen and slow to speak (James 1:19). This principle works in many kinds of relational settings, but it is especially true when it comes to Witness-Life. In *I Once Was Lost* by Don Everts and Doug Schaupp, the authors tell us Jesus was asked 183 questions throughout the Gospels. He answered only three of them! Far more often, He asked questions and answered questions with questions. In fact, He did that 307 times.

I confess that I imagine Jesus speaking to crowds a lot more than I think of Him engaging with individuals, but in fact He engaged individuals often. Sometimes He asked questions that at first have seemingly no spiritual connotation. His first words to the woman at the well were, "Will you give me a drink?" (John 4:7). We know where that led. He asked a paralyzed man, "Do you want to get well?" (5:6). On both occasions God was doing something significant in their lives of which they weren't aware. Jesus engaged people right where they lived. While talking with Nicodemus, who came to Him secretly in the night, Jesus had a long discussion about spiritual things. In the course of the conversation, Jesus asked this theologian two challenging questions, "You are Israel's teacher . . . and do you not understand these things?" (3:10). The next question was even more penetrating. He said, "I have spoken to you of earthly things and you do not believe; how then will you believe if I speak of heavenly things?" (v. 12). I encourage you to take a fresh look at the four Gospels and note how often Jesus asked questions.

AS WE ENGAGE PEOPLE IN SPIRITUAL CONVERSATION, GOD OFTEN LETS US KNOW HE IS AT WORK BY THE DEGREE OF INTEREST THE PERSON SHOWS.

It seems Paul and Peter noticed this and adopted it in their lives as well. In two impactful passages, we see both Paul and Peter point out the importance of listening and asking questions. Paul wrote, "Let your conversation be always full of grace, seasoned with salt, so that you may know how to answer everyone" (Colossians 4:6). He assumes our witness is conversational. He enjoins us to be loving (graceful) and winsome with our words. But note the big surprise. He ends the passage by stating we need to know how to answer everyone. Answers can't be given until a question has been asked! As we engage people in spiritual conversation, God often lets us know He is at work by the degree of interest the person shows. That interest is best measured by the listener asking questions.

Peter followed the same line of reasoning.

> *Always be prepared to give an answer to everyone who asks you to give the reason for the hope that you have. But do this with gentleness and respect.*
> —1 Peter 3:15

He asks us to be ready to explain our faith when people are curious about it. He assumed people would be asking. And of course, he is right. Remember: God is the evangelist, and He draws people toward Himself. He invites us into the conversations He is already having with people who are far from Him. Questions will be asked, and like Paul, Peter asks us to be gentle and respectful in our dialogue and responses.

Can you remember a time when you felt really listened to? It is such a gift. I have a colleague with a special listening capacity. His name is Bill. His eyes are intense and full of love whenever you speak with him. His body leans into a conversation with full attention. I don't recall Bill ever talking over me or interrupting.

REMEMBER: GOD IS THE EVANGELIST, AND HE DRAWS PEOPLE TOWARD HIMSELF. HE INVITES US INTO THE CONVERSATIONS HE IS ALREADY HAVING WITH PEOPLE WHO ARE FAR FROM HIM.

He silently and attentively listens. There aren't many Bills. His example makes me want to listen better to my wife (whom I just cut off in midsentence—*ugh!*) and all the people I know and meet. Our ability to deeply listen is undoubtedly impacted by the speed of our lives.

In his book *Tranquility*, David Henderson says that cardiologists have a phrase to define a chronic sense of time urgency that many of their patients display—"hurry sickness." Those who study this sickness note dangerous symptoms, including "racing-mind syndrome," which results in an inability to focus on anyone or anything. Our need to slow down the rapid pace of our lives is heightened as we realize a hectic life will hinder us from listening to people looking for Him.

The man in Israel leading our mission into the Arab-Muslim towns told us we should ready ourselves to drink a lot of strong coffee and eat a lot of food over long periods of time. In his culture, the love of friendship and relationships includes a near disregard of time constraints. We are entering people's lives, listening for open doors in conversation, and it will require more time than we are conditioned to give. This will be quite a test for Americans on the edge of "hurry sickness." It's not a sacrifice on our part. It is exposing an acute weakness in the average American's lifestyle namely, "racing-mind syndrome."

Listening has a second dimension as well. Share 1 requires we learn how to hear God and how to hear the people with whom we are engaging. God actively provides our witness appointments and guides them once we arrive. Thank goodness He doesn't send us to the appointments alone! This means we are listening in prayer with God as we are listening to the person(s) in front of us. Since God is with us (Matthew 28:20), and since the salvation of souls is His first priority, it makes sense to believe He guides us in what we say.

I'm not really good at listening to both God and the person I'm speaking with, but I'm getting better. Offering silent prayers for guidance is all that is required. There are a lot of occasions when a lull occurs or I don't know what to say in response to a question. A silent prayer becomes urgent in those times. God is faithful. He will provide. It's incumbent on us to trust that He is speaking into our minds, and we can follow our intuition in such moments. It really can—and does—work.

I remember a few short years ago when a couple came forward for prayer after a sermon. They'd been sitting in the front row, which is usually a sign of a very engaged and devoted Christian. I was serving as a prayer counselor that day, and the wife began to pour out her problem. As I listened to her, I had the intuitive sense that God was speaking to me as I listened. I felt Him saying the woman's problem was secondary. Her relationship with Him was first. I acted on the intuitive lead and said something like, "I want to listen more to what you are saying, but may I ask a question first?" She gladly nodded yes. Then I jumped. "Have you ever committed your life to Jesus Christ and invited Him in your life? You really need Him in order to come through this issue." She paused and looked straight at me. Then she said, "No, I haven't ever done that." I responded, "Would you like to?" She said, "Yes, I would."

God interrupted my listening and directed the conversation where it needed to go. The woman was clearly convicted of her alienation from God and converted and regenerated that day. Today she and her husband are deeply active and growing in marvelous ways. It makes me smile to think about them. Perhaps you have had similar experiences. It has been a continual learning experience for me to listen both to God and the person I'm speaking with. If I can do it, so can you. It is so fulfilling to be used by God to open up spiritual dialogue with someone.

STAGES IN CONVERSATION

A conversation of listening and asking questions seldom starts at a serious or very personal level. Most are peripheral before personal. This is true with people we know and with strangers. It's actually inappropriate in most cultures to start a conversation with a person at a deep level, and since spiritual discussions are deep and personal, we don't want to start there. Consider the three stages of conversation:

— STAGE 1: PERIPHERAL QUESTIONS —

1. Check-in questions: "How are you doing?" Or in the United Kingdom, they ask, "You all right?"

2. Weather questions: "Isn't it a beautiful day?" "Isn't it cold?" Universally, starting conversation around the weather is a winner.

3. News or sports questions: "How about those Cubs?" "Isn't this election cycle crazy?"

4. Greeting: "Hello! How are you?" That's right. Just greeting someone often opens up human interaction!

Conversations can continue in a peripheral or impersonal way for quite a while. There is nothing wrong with that. It is part of the joy of being human and needing any kind of interpersonal touch. Sometimes men who are talking about sports or cars can do so for hours without end. Right now I can see my neighbor out our back windows. It is the day before Easter, and it is a lovely day. If I walk outside, Hank and I would talk about the weather and how nice it is to see the grass greening before the end of March. Since he is seeding his lawn, we would talk about how long it will be before we need to mow. We'd probably wish each other a happy Easter and go back to our business. In fact, I'm going to go speak to him right now . . .

Sure enough, Hank is well, though just getting over an awful flu, which set him back at work a lot. He is putting crab grass fertilizer on his lawn and doing it now because it may rain tonight. We are both surprised the grass has turned green so early. We did wish each other a happy Easter. That was it, and that was enjoyable. Hank and his wife are wonderful neighbors, and even talking on the impersonal level is pleasing.

— STAGE 2: PERSONAL QUESTIONS —

If a conversation goes beyond the peripheral, it usually starts getting personal. This is especially true when there is already a personal friendship established. With such people, we can dive deeper within a few minutes. With strangers, it is longer but no less meaningful. Here are some good questions to move from the peripheral to the personal:

 Work and hobby questions: "Tell me about your work.

Is it going well?" If talking to a stranger, you could ask, "How long have you been in that kind of work?" "Do you enjoy your work?" "What is most meaningful about your work or your hobbies?" "What do you like doing when there is nothing you must do?"

2. Family questions: "How is your family?" When I'm on an airplane, I often ask where the person is heading. If they are heading home, the conversation often leads to family questions. "Do you have any children?" If I notice a wedding ring I ask, "How long have you been married?"

3. Health questions: "How are you feeling since the surgery?" "Is your mother better?"

4. Cultural crisis questions: "Are you following the events since Sandy Hook Elementary, or Paris, or San Bernardino, or Brussels . . . ?" (Sadly, this list never ends.)

These kinds of questions and topics of conversation take us into the world of the personal. With people we know, a degree of trust has to be achieved before others will honestly address them. Sometimes, with strangers, one can get to the personal quickly since there is some protection if it's a person you know you won't see again. Sitting on an airplane for several hours with a total stranger can sometimes do that.

When we get personal, we are impacting people and being impacted where life matters and hits hardest. My neighbor Hank and I spoke for less than ten minutes, but in that time we moved quickly from the peripheral to the personal. Our relationship is one of trust, respect, and history—so it happens. I learned he recently recovered from a severe bout of the flu, and he remembered we just celebrated the birth of our first grandchild. That led him, because he is a medical professional, to talk about the wonder and mystery of holding a newborn child. This is personal stuff, and this is the time when it is appropriate and natural to introduce spiritual discussion.

— STAGE 3: PERSONAL SPIRITUAL QUESTIONS —

Many people have told me they have no problems talking about God and Jesus with people but that they don't know how to get it started! How do we start God-talk and discern whether the person has any spiritual interest or curiosity? That is a great question. It's not easy, and this is a good moment to remember what we discussed in the beginning of the chapter on listening to God and praying for guidance.

I use a principle called the "ten-minute rule." I learned this many years ago from a pastor who said he felt no compulsion to suggest spiritual conversation with a friend, acquaintance, or stranger, until he'd talked with the person for at least ten minutes. Usually within ten minutes a conversation has moved from the peripheral to the personal, which makes introducing the idea of God into conversation more appropriate.

> TO BRING GOD UP WHEN A CONVERSATION IS VERY IMPERSONAL OR PERIPHERAL IS UNWISE AND OFTEN JUST SILLY.

The ten-minute rule also takes the pressure off to feel like you have to witness with everyone you meet. I used to feel that kind of pressure, but no longer. To bring God up when a conversation is very impersonal or peripheral is unwise and often just silly. Let me illustrate. If I were talking with Hank and mentioned what a beautiful warm day it is for March and immediately followed up with, "Oh, by the way, you want to talk about heat, hell is hot. If you don't receive Jesus, you'll burn." That is as inappropriate as meeting a stranger and asking how much money they make or being with a married couple over a casual dinner and asking about their sex life. You just don't and shouldn't do that. The ten-minute rule sets the table for appropriate conversation around things that matter.

Here are a few questions that can start God-talk:

1. For strangers: "Do you have a church home?" "Do you have any religious or spiritual background?" "Are you interested in spirituality?"

2. For strangers or FRANs: "Do you ever think about God?" "Do you feel like God loves you?" "Do you think God is good?" "Did you go to your church on Easter/ Christmas?"

3. "Is there anything I can pray for you about?" (The offer of prayer has tremendous impact on all people. I'm sure Marie and I have asked this question several hundred times. Ninety-nine percent of the time, the person says yes and tells us of a need.)

4. "Where are you on your spiritual journey?" (This

question was given to me recently by Dr. Erwin Lutzer from Moody Memorial Church. He says he uses it often and it has opened numerous doors.)

 After you engage in spiritual conversation and sense definite interest from your friend: "If you knew you could have a personal relationship with God, would you be interested?"

HUMAN LONGING

Once a conversation becomes personal, it usually awakens true human longings. We all have them. These longings were placed in us by our Creator and only find their satisfaction in Him. Ecclesiastes declares He has put eternity in our hearts (Ecclesiastes 3:11). Like a beacon on the sea, He draws us toward Himself. Our longings for Christ and home can represent themselves in many ways. I've been very drawn to the writings of N. T. Wright on this matter. In his excellent book, *Simply Christian*, he speaks of four "echoes of a voice" inherent in all people. Echoes of a voice refers to the longings God has placed in human hearts. It is similar to the term "inconsolable longings" first discussed by C. S. Lewis. Wright's sense is that every human being at their core desires justice, beauty, love, and God.

LIKE A BEACON ON THE SEA, HE DRAWS US TOWARD HIMSELF.

A few years after he wrote *Simply Christian*, I had the opportunity to be with Dr. Wright and a few others. I asked if he had added any echoes. He said yes, the human longing for freedom. He spent time in countries where there was little personal freedom and saw how people longed for it. I personally believe there is a sixth. I believe the human need for purpose is universal. If we list those together, they look like:

1 Justice—for self and all the world

2 Beauty—attraction to creation, art, humanity

3 Love—to be cared for and to care

4 God—an inner spiritual drawing to the divine

5 Freedom—to have personal choice, political and economic liberties, etc.

6 Purpose—to have a reason for existence, to matter

Recently two significant pastors and theologians brought a fresh look at this subject. In his book *Center Church*, Tim Keller discusses D. A. Carson's eight motivations to implement when appealing to non-Christians to believe the gospel. The list interacts some with Wright's but has unique elements as well. Keller lists and summarizes six of those motivations, which I've included below.

1 Fear of judgment and death

2 Release from guilt and shame

3 Attractiveness of truth

4 Existential longings—inner joy and peace, hope, etc., that can be experienced now

Help in crisis and despair

 To be loved

Following is my attempt to summarize the two lists. This summary will be important as you begin to see and hear these longings in people you listen to. When it comes to moving from Share 1 to Share 2, which is telling our own story, I will ask you to identify one or more of these longings that God used to draw you to Himself.

— SUMMARY OF HUMAN LONGINGS —
(based on Wright, Keller, and Carson)

1 Forever life—longing for eternal life and happiness

2 Truth—longing for meaning

3 Forgiveness—longing for an answer to guilt and shame

4 Help—longing for something or someone that can help us in our suffering and the world in crisis

5 Relationships—longing to not be alone

6 Beauty—longing for what is lovely and good

7 God—longing for an eternal being who is lovely, good, and in control

8 Freedom—longing for power to break the evil within the world and self

9 Purpose—longing to matter in this world

10 Justice—longing for all that is wrong to be made right

11 Peace, Happiness, Contentment—longing to feel calm, secure, and good about life

12 Hope—longing to believe things will be better, no matter how bad they are

This list is not exhaustive, but I'm convinced these 12 longings touch humans everywhere. When you talk with people at deep levels, one or many of these surface. The wise and prayerful believer committed to Share-Witness will recognize these longings and stimulate conversation around them. Each of these longings is a pathway to the heart, where only the true gospel of our Lord Jesus Christ can fill the emptiness and fear.

I close this chapter with the words of an American rock poet by the name of Paul Simon. In his classic song, "American Tune," he sings:

> *I don't know a soul who's not been battered,*
>
> *I don't have a friend who feels at ease,*
>
> *I don't know a dream that's not been shattered,*
>
> *Or driven to its knees.*

Human beings long to find answers to the deep inconsolable places in their lives. This is our calling—to bring the message of Christ to them. Remember our Lord's words on the last day of the great feast. "Let anyone who is thirsty come to me and drink. Whoever believes in me, as Scripture has said, rivers of living water will flow from within them" (John 7:37–38). Living water, quenched thirst, the God-shaped vacuum, the restless heart, inconsolable longings, echoes of a voice—all point to His words, "Come to me." You may be saying to yourself something like this, "But, Lon, coming to Jesus is more than getting our deep needs met. It requires confessing before Almighty God our sin of self-worship and turning away from sins of thought, word, deed, and the like." I agree with you 100 percent. But most people don't start there. They start their faith journey looking for a God to help where they experience their hurt. Felt needs are the pathway to the human heart. God then takes them to the deeper need of reconciling with Him. It is a process. Share 1 starts to reveal those things to both the seeker and to you, the witness God has brought to them at this moment in his or her life.

These are the kinds of things we learn as we enter into Share-Witness. Peripheral conversation becomes personal conversation and personal leads to spiritual or God-talk. What a privilege to be partners with God to listen and inquire into the stories of people's lives! What an honor and sacred responsibility to offer God's love to searching and aching human hearts!

CHAPTER 9

Share 2
Our Stories

JEFF is an elder in our church. He has a beautiful family, a wonderful business, and a severe cancer that, by the grace and mercy of God, is in miraculous remission. Just a week ago, Jeff was with me in Israel, along with several other church members. Applying Luke 9:1–6 and 10:1–12 literally, we asked God to enable us to meet Arab Muslim people and share Jesus Christ and His saving message with them. We drove into villages of 500–5,000 people and parked our vans briefly for prayer. We asked God to lead us to someone who would be open to receiving strangers for conversation and coffee. Eight times in eight towns, God led us to someone. Our Christian Arab partner would roll down the window of our van when we spotted a man walking on his street or in the front of his home, and he'd ask, "I have some Americans who would like to meet you and your family. Would you like coffee?" The response was always yes, and usually enthusiastically so!

Before we knew it, the hosts would set up plastic chairs for the 12 of us and his family and friends. Arabic coffee would be served, along with orange and grape soda most of the time. Conversation began with our Arab brother translating. Before long more family members would join and sometimes neighbors. Hospitality is a deeply treasured value in Arab cultures. Work ceases when friends or guests appear. Often food would be served to us. Olives, hummus, unleavened bread, local vegetables, and more, would be placed on makeshift tables. The conversation was of the Share 1 variety. Talk moved from peripheral to personal. Then, because Arab Muslims are inherently religious people and because we'd already shared that we had come as pilgrims to meet people and visit holy sites, it flowed easily to personal spiritual sharing. This is when Jeff almost always took the lead.

How do we move from Share I and personal spiritual questions and dialogue to expressing our own love for Christ? The very best way is by telling our own stories of how Jesus Christ has been and is real to us. It is far easier to tell people how and why we've come to know and love Jesus Christ than it is to tell them they should. This is exactly what Jeff did. He knew and we knew that Muslims and Christians hold different theological views of God and Jesus. And, quite honestly, if Jeff or I brought up those theological differences, the conversation would've no doubt ended in arguments and disharmony. But when Jeff told his story of how Jesus Christ had brought healing to his body and even more to his soul, there was rapt attention.

A PERSONAL STORY WILL ALMOST ALWAYS DO MORE THAN A SERMON OR A LECTURE.

A personal story will almost always do more than a sermon or a lecture. In fact, as a professor in the field of Christian preaching, I teach storytelling as an integral part of all effective preaching. Jeff didn't preach or lecture. He simply told his story, and it only took a few minutes. His story crossed cultures in a split second because all people long for help in times of need. The crisis of cancer hits everywhere. The hope for healing is universal. It doesn't matter if one is American, Arab, or any other nationality. Our stories of God's work in our lives capture attention.

I believe the soul is made for stories as much as the body is made for water and food. It's always been that way. I've learned a lot about the importance of story and how to tell stories through a former Fulbright Scholar and one of the world's premier screenwriting teachers, Robert McKee. In his book *Story*, McKee quotes literary theorist Kenneth Burke in saying, "Stories are the equipment for living." Stories have the capacity to awaken emotions and memories. Stories create a sense of community even among strangers. Stories remind us how much we have in common as human beings. And it is through stories that the ideas and meanings of things take hold, find definition, and are remembered. That's why, since the beginning of time, around cook fires and around kitchen tables today, human beings communicate and connect because of stories.

> I BELIEVE THE SOUL IS MADE FOR STORIES AS MUCH AS THE BODY IS MADE FOR WATER AND FOOD.

I encourage you to think back over the last 24 hours. What do you remember? Chances are pretty good you remember events more than you do ideas from the day. Why? Because the things that happen to you become your stories. And your ideas are derived from those stories and events. Then, they are contained, remembered, and given meaning within the events or stories. Those events become the stories of your life.

As I think back over my last 24 hours, I remember our son calling from California. It surprised us since we'd not heard from him for a few weeks. We'd been increasingly concerned about some issues in his life, one of which was the lack of contact with us. I could delineate the rest of those issues, but they wouldn't be very interesting. What might be interesting, however, is how the call put our minds at rest. Why? Because our son brought up the issues we were concerned about before we brought them up.

And, he was working through them in a mature way. God was so faithful to us—a worrying dad and mom of a twentysomething adult child. Today, I'm full of thanksgiving to God.

What was our takeaway or the big truth in the story? Namely, God was the Father to our son when I could not be because of distance and personality. God was and is sufficient. That event with our son is now a story; it was not stored in my mind as a set of ideas or parental principles. In fact, I can only remember the ideas or principles because I've linked them in my mind to the story of the telephone call. I remember my whole life, and almost everything I remember I know through my recollection of the stories of my life. You probably do as well.

If stories have so much value to our souls, then we shouldn't be surprised to see how much of the Bible is contained in stories. As I take a look at the 66 books of the Bible, I see that more than half of its pages are in story or narrative form. Nearly three quarters of the New Testament are in story form, including 90 percent of the four Gospels. Perhaps most meaningful is to see the value and weight our Lord Jesus gave to story and narrative in His teaching. Read Eugene Peterson's paraphrase of the following text in *The Message* as he takes the word *parable* and calls it what it is—story:

> *All Jesus did that day was tell stories—a long storytelling afternoon. His storytelling fulfilled the prophecy: I will open my mouth and tell stories; I will bring out into the open things hidden since the world's first day.*
> —Matthew 13:34–35

Earlier in the chapter, the disciples asked Jesus why He told so many stories. Jesus responded:

> *You've been given insight into God's kingdom. You know how it works. Not everybody has this gift, this insight; it hasn't been given to them . . . That's why I tell stories: to create readiness, to nudge the people toward receptive insight.*
> —Matthew 13:11–13 *The Message*

Let's talk about the ways we can use our stories of God's work in our lives to help create readiness and nudge people toward receptive insight. Share 1 conversation with people gives us understanding of their stories and worlds. Sometimes Share 1 goes on for only a few minutes. Other times it can go on for hours, days, or even years in unraveling episodes, depending on whether we are engaged with strangers or FRANs. But if and when Share 1 talking moves into personal spiritual issues, it is the perfect time to move toward Share 2 and offer personal spiritual stories from our lives. Sometimes they flow naturally into the conversation.

Often in my life, if I'm talking with a person about spiritual things and they tell me some of their stories and views of spiritual life, I can assume they will be open to hearing stories from my life as well. For instance, if a person has just told me about their religious background or lack thereof, I can simply say, "That's an interesting story, mine is that I grew up in a nonspiritual home . . ." Then I give a brief synopsis of my background and how I came to experience a personal relationship with Jesus Christ.

Sometimes a transitional question sets the table for you to share. For instance, after a person tells you their spiritual background story, you can ask, "May I take a couple of minutes to tell you my background?" Almost always they will agree. If they don't have time, are uninterested, or worse, put you off with a cavalier attitude, you simply respect their feelings, pray for another opportunity, and leave the present moment in God's hands.

When God opens the door for you to tell your story, you have two kinds of spiritual stories at your disposal.

JOURNEY WITH JESUS STORIES

Every Christian has Journey with Jesus stories galore. What are they? A Journey with Jesus story is a quick telling of ways you see God at work in your everyday life. I tell believers to take the same stories they praise God for in their prayers or share with their Christian friends and repackage them in ways prebelievers can understand. That makes them a Journey with Jesus story. These are especially valuable with FRANs. If we know them and they know we are Christians, they will expect that we will share life from our worldview. Jesus said we are not to leave our light under a bowl. Instead we put it on a stand so that it gives light to all (see Matthew 5:15). Very often Christians put their lights under bowls and don't talk about God with non-God-oriented people for fear of offending them. We need not do that. Just as they talk of life from their worldview, so can we.

I am not a fan of the Chicago White Sox baseball team. I don't dislike them, but I don't go out of my way to follow them. My good friend and neighbor loves the White Sox. He talks about them all throughout baseball season. He doesn't shove them down my throat. He doesn't make me watch them on television or make me go to a game with him. He simply includes them in his summertime conversations. I get that and can respect it. I actually like that about him. He's a great guy, and whenever I'm around him, I start liking the White Sox a little bit more. However, I really long for him to know and trust Jesus. Well, since Jesus is the most important reality in my life in every season, of course I am going to talk about Him and ways He helps me in my life or how I see His greatness in the warmth of summer or in the coming of spring after a Chicago winter. My friend talks baseball, and I look for open doors to talk about God sightings in my life. The sooner a Christian gets his or her Christian worldview on the table when meeting people or carrying on casual friendships with relatives, neighbors, and work associates, the better. I do that with my neighbor. I expect the White Sox from him, and he expects Journey with Jesus stories from me.

JOURNEY WITH JESUS STORIES ARE WONDERFUL AND SIMPLE, AUTHENTIC WAYS TO WITNESS OF GOD'S GOODNESS AND SOVEREIGNTY.

Journey with Jesus stories are wonderful and simple, authentic ways to witness of God's goodness and sovereignty. They can be very brief, about little things, or about big things. Just last weekend I walked out to get our newspaper and saw our neighbors across the street working in their yard—it's finally starting to get warm in Chicago. I walked over to their home with the newspaper under my arm and simply said something like, "Isn't God good? We are about to enter the happy days of warmth." That was it. It wasn't a calculated response. It was really just thanksgiving and praise put into everyday conversation.

The next day I was getting a haircut. Shirley has cut my hair for nearly ten years. In those 15 minutes of haircutting (I don't have much hair to cut!), we always have some conversation that gets to the personal areas of family. I've met her son and husband and know some about her parents. She knows Marie and knows about our children. So in our conversation I said, "Shirley, our daughter had her baby five weeks ago. I'm a grand-dad." She was, of course, congratulatory. Then I said something like, "When I held little Aubrey in my arms only a few hours after her birth I was in awe. She had ten fingers, ten toes, and every piece in place in miniature form. I found myself thinking how wonderful the Creator God is to design such a thing as a baby." Then I said, "How could anyone believe little Aubrey is the result of mere chance?" That was it. She affirmed my words. Shirley is a believer in God but not a devoted follower yet. My purpose was merely to bring the reality of God into our conversation and allow Him to use the story to draw her one step closer to Himself.

In both of these cases, there has been several years of casual relationship. I've sought to go deeper with both, and the doors have not yet been opened fully. But Journey with Jesus stories are tailor-made for people in the early stages of spiritual exploration. Some journey stories are simple and small. Some are powerful and profound. God uses them all. Go back to the One Step Closer to Christ Spiritual Journey Chart in chapter 3. Journey with Jesus stories are especially helpful for people in the beginning and midrange stages of the journey toward Christ. My neighbors, Shirley, and the Arab-Muslim strangers we ministered to in Israel all fit into those spaces. We have Journey with Jesus stories all the time. They are a part of our daily journey with God, and God intends them to be a link between people He is calling to Himself.

Here is my challenge, and it's eminently doable. Go back in your memory banks just 24 hours. Was there an event of small or large impact where you clearly saw God at work? You probably already thanked Him for it in your prayers or devotions. Our son's surprising telephone call was one of mine, as well my conversations with my neighbors and Shirley. If nothing comes to mind, then go back to the last week. There you will find several potential Journey with Jesus stories wrapped in praise and thanksgiving.

Take the time to write down one or two of them. Try to keep them short, no longer than 200 words. Writing them down will awaken your memory to retain them for the future. Finally, ask God for the opportunity to share one or more of them with someone on your prayer list this week. You can do that by conversation, a text or social media entry, or even via voice mail. Once you establish this practice, you'll find a way to share them often. They will give you great joy. Soon, you won't need to write them out as you develop the practice and find them readied in your memory, cataloged and called forward by God whenever He warrants. It is so much fun to tell people how God is at work in our lives and world.

CONVERTING STORIES

Converting stories describe how we came to know Christ or reaffirmed our childhood faith in Christ. These are often commonly referred to as our testimonies. The purpose of Converting stories is to help people see their lives can change by coming to know Jesus Christ personally, just as we have. These are stories of great importance to us—defining moments, if you will. They are the stories of life's great journey to discover God. I don't want to be too severe here, but having these Converting stories deeply ingrained in our memories and easily recalled to share is as important for the soul as CPR training is to resuscitating a body. OK, so maybe that's severe, but there is truth in it. There is really no excuse for any Christ follower to not be able to tell the story of how God found and saved them.

THIS HAS CONVINCED ME FOR MANY YEARS THAT MY ELOQUENCE AND THEOLOGICAL PRECISION MATTER FAR LESS THAN THE MERE TELLING OF THE STORIES OF HOW GOD REMADE MY LIFE AND SAVED ME FOR ETERNITY WITH HIM.

The Apostle Paul certainly saw the importance of his Converting story. He called it his defense (Acts 26:1–2). The Greek word for *defense* is where we get the word *apologetics*, a word that literally means "defense." His Converting story was his best defense, or proof, of the truth of Christianity. He used his conversion story as a defense at least three times in the Book of Acts: before an angry mob (22:1–21), a Roman governor (24:10–21), and a king and queen (26:1–30). All who have studied the great apostle's life know of his brilliant mind and his deep fullness of the Holy Spirit. Before each of those audiences, he could've spoken mysteries and theological wonders. Yet on each occasion, he chose not to teach reasoned doctrine but the story of his own changed life. This has convinced me for many years that my eloquence and theological precision matter far less than the mere telling of the stories of how God remade my life and saved me for eternity with Him.

On the One Step Closer to Christ Spiritual Journey Chart in chapter 3, Converting stories are especially important and relevant for people coming closer to Christ that are at least at a stage -8. They are for people at the place of thinking deeply about coming to Christ. By all appearances the Holy Spirit is drawing them in. However, since we don't always know how close a person is and since God alone does the saving, we should have our Converting stories ready for anyone who is interested, whether a complete stranger who is curious or a close relative who has expressed deep interest in God.

You have a Converting story. You may well have more than one like me, and you're not completely sure when you converted and were regenerated by the Holy Spirit. Over the years, I realized some Christians trace their conversion to a clear and memorable point in time. They can tell you the day and sometimes the hour of when they, to the best of their knowledge, surrendered the control of their lives to Jesus and experienced new birth.

Others cannot point to an exact time or occasion. Their stories, usually comprised of having been raised in a Christian home, have more to do with experiencing Christians and the Christ-life from an early age. Many have no recollection of ever not believing in Christ. This is often the case with believers nurtured in a place where evangelical Christianity has a firm foothold. For such people, it is not a point in time, but a period of time as love for Jesus progresses and grows. Nearly half of those I've trained identify with this type of Converting story, though that percentage is dropping as we train more people from unchurched backgrounds. Both avenues are valid stories and bring great glory to our Lord and King.

Billy Graham traces his conversion to a point in time when he walked forward at a Mordecai Ham crusade in Charlotte, North Carolina, in his teens. His wife, Ruth, however, doesn't remember ever not believing in Christ. Ruth Graham grew up in the loving nurture of a missionary home in China. Both her parents loved the Lord with all their hearts, and Ruth did as well from early childhood. Like a flower her faith flourished and grew into beauty.

I liken this to the tulips in our front yard. The green stems started growing slowly again as the winter cold was replaced by sunny days. Then quite suddenly one day, bright red flowers appeared. It all happened over a period of time. The plants were stems yesterday, and bright red tulips this morning.

I often hear people with a period-of-time type of story say they don't have a testimony or Converting story. That is incorrect. What they really mean is that they don't have what is in their minds a compelling story with a clear starting point. They, in fact, have a blessed and beautiful story of being aware of God even as a child and learning about Christ and His life when trusting God is as easy as trusting one's parents. We can't ever forget that children who are drawn to Jesus have a very special place in His kingdom. He said, "Let the little children come to me, and do not hinder them, for the kingdom of heaven belongs to such as these" (Matthew 19:14). If your Converting story is of this type, be grateful. You possess a level of love and trust in Jesus that makes me a bit envious. Further, I've found that people far from God are actually very interested in hearing stories of people nurtured in loving homes with Christian faith. Tell your story whichever it is, and watch God use it!

Fortunately we have wonderful examples in Scripture of these two types of Converting stories. The Apostle Paul represents the point-in-time Converting story and his disciple Timothy the period-of-time story. Note this, however: the Timothy-like period-of-time stories usually have an event or two over time during which the believer, through either conviction or crisis, steps more fully into their faith. Some have called this moving from the faith of their parents to adult faith. I promise to give lots of guidance on how to shape your Converting stories into meaningful and impacting offerings.

— POINT-IN-TIME —

In Acts 26, Paul shares his Converting story with King Agrippa, his wife Bernice, and the Roman governor, Festus. His Converting story is divided into three parts:

Before—His life before meeting Jesus Christ (Acts 26: 4–11)

How—His encounter with Jesus Christ (Acts 26: 12–18)

Now—His life since meeting Jesus Christ (Acts 26: 19–23)

I summarize this clear and easy-to-follow outline with three words: *before*, *how*, and *now*. For all readers who see their Converting stories as a point in time, this is your outline. Let's talk a bit about timing. If you read Paul's story and can imagine that we don't have it word for word from Luke, author of the Book of Acts, but instead read a summary there, you realize it was quite long. Yours and mine should not be that long. Paul was a master communicator, skilled in all phases of rhetoric. Most of us are not. Further, in this setting he was asked to give a full defense in a forum. That is not the setting for most of us. I have found it helpful to limit my story to two minutes. You should too. I know that seems short, but the truth is most occasions for sharing are in conversational settings, not in speech settings. If you can learn to tell your story in two minutes, you can expand it when appropriate.

This happened to me while I was on the missions trip in Israel. Nearly 150 Arab Muslims were at a banquet and I, as the elder American, was asked to explain why God and Jesus Christ were so important to me. Following Paul's lead, I gave my two-minute Converting story and expanded it to about ten. Since I was also being translated into Arabic, it actually became about 20 minutes. God honored His Word through the words of a human voice, and nearly 20 Muslims asked for prayer following it. It may be that a few became Christ followers. It's hard to tell in such a setting because Muslims who convert to Christ must be very careful when and how they publicly declare faith in Jesus because of possible cultural and societal repercussions.

I took my two-minute story and expanded it for the public speech occasion at hand. If, however, you prepare your story in its lengthier form, chances are it will be less compelling because most people in conversational settings won't listen to a long story. Longer stories can often be unclear and less impactful. Preparing a shorter story first and diligently editing it to be clear and succinct means it can be expanded to maintain clarity and poignancy. So, let's settle on two-minute stories—which means no more than 300 words. Here are my two Converting stories:

— EXAMPLE 1 —

I was a typical California kid raised on the Beatles, Beach Boys, and Bob Dylan. The music and the whole counter-cultural movement of the late 1960s awakened a deep loneliness in me and told me I'd only be fulfilled when I found the right girl for my life.

Well, I met a lovely dark-haired beauty and found the songs were all true! It was wonderful . . . for about three months. Then she quite suddenly broke up with me for a college guy. My heart was smashed into pieces, and I was filled with sadness and anger because I felt betrayed.

Some friends who were followers of Jesus surrounded me in that time and began to tell me about a living Jesus who could enter my aloneness and that He would never leave me or betray me. I still remember the night when I took a chance and, laying in my bed, asked Him to be my God, my Leader, and my Friend. I learned He would also forgive all the wrongs of my life.

That was nearly 40 years ago. Today, my life is filled with Him through His personal presence and His gifts of a wonderful wife, family, and friends. I am not alone. Most of all, He kept His promise to love me, forgive me, and never leave me. I'm deeply grateful. I now spend my life telling other people about Him and offering them the same wonderful relationship with God that was offered me so long ago.

— EXAMPLE 2 —

I needed God more than I imagined possible. Underneath my life as a 19 year old was an enormous ache, a guilt so embedded it paralyzed me in some ways. You see, when I was 13, my little two-year-old brother drowned. It happened late one afternoon. He'd been watching my friends and me play baseball down around the corner from our home. I remember yelling at him to go home because I didn't want him there. He left, went home without my mother knowing, and got into our backyard. While playing with his toy trucks, he fell into our swimming pool and died. I always felt it was my fault and that my family, the world, and God (though I didn't know much about Him) should blame me. I needed to be rescued.

At 19, I suffered from serious chronic intestinal pain. I was placed in the hospital, where for three weeks doctors searched for and eventually found a bleeding ulcer.

The physical pain and uncertainty of those days were used by God to unlock my deep inner ache. One night while in the hospital, a local Christian youth leader came to visit. I poured out the story of my brother to him. As I wept, he told me about Jesus dying on the Cross and helped me hear Jesus say from the Cross, "Father, forgive him, he didn't know what he was doing." I felt a rush of forgiveness and inner relief flood my heart.

Jesus gave His life to rescue me. I am forgiven and await the day I'll join my brother and Jesus in heaven. Until that time, I am called to rescue others with the same truth that rescued me. I am eternally grateful.

In both of those stories, I sought to use Paul's method of life before Christ, how he encountered Christ, and life now with Christ.

— PERIOD-OF-TIME —

The life of Timothy provides a framework for a "period-of-time" Converting story and works for Christians who remember their spiritual birth journey occurring over a period of time, increasing in commitment as time progressed. This framework can also be divided into three parts:

Before—His early life with Christ (2 Timothy 1:5; 3:15)

How—His deeper encounter with Christ (2 Timothy 1:6)

Now—His life since the encounter with Christ
(2 Timothy 4:2, 5)

These passages tell us a lot about Timothy. They are a minibiography of him told by his mentor, Paul. In the first season of life, he was bathed in Scripture. His mother and grandmother nurtured him. We even know their names—Eunice and Lois— and that they were women of sincere faith. What a privilege and grace to be raised in such a home. Note, however, Paul doesn't say their true faith was also Timothy's. He says, it is *now* (2 Timothy 1:5). This is a clue that Timothy may've had a journey to deep encounter with faith in Christ. We don't know exactly what occurred, but in 2 Timothy 1:6, we get a hint of something. Paul entered into Timothy's life, and at a certain time his faith was fanned into flame through the laying on of Paul's hands. Did Timothy have a nominal or casual faith until that time? Perhaps. Did he have a crisis of faith? Perhaps. We don't know. What is clear, however, is that this young man raised in a faith-driven household had a "deeper" event, a kind of tipping point when his faith was set on fire. Often such events happen at Christian events, camps, or revivals.

My daughter, who had a Timothy-like early life, had a dream encounter with Jesus in college that fanned her faith into flame. Like many kids raised in Christian households, her faith needed to become her own, and for several years, it was not. In the dream, God told her He had an important purpose for her life and that she should not waste her life on her own desires but live her life for His desires. From that day on, she's been a fully devoted Christ follower.

God calls His beloved children deeper to Him in all sorts of ways. If you have a period of time Converting story, ask the Lord to take you back and remind you of an event (or several) that led you to your fully devoted faith. I bet you'll find something. You'll probably find it is linked to one of the soul longings I wrote about in chapter 8.

As for Timothy, his past led to an impacting present (Now). He served as a pastor in Ephesus, one of the major crossroads cities of the world. From there all of Asia was hearing the gospel (Acts 19:10). Paul describes Timothy's calling and mentors him in his strategic role of preacher and evangelist in the two biblical letters bearing Timothy's name.

If you are reading this book and have a Timothy-like period-of-time Converting story, I imagine you too are serving Jesus fully. It is time for you to get in touch with your story and develop it in such a way that God can use it in many lives. As with the point-in-time Converting stories, I recommend you craft it according to the scriptural model of *Before*, *How*, and *Now* that we see in Timothy's journey. Work on it carefully, and keep it less than 300 words so you can deliver it in two minutes or less. But before you do, read the following fictionalized examples. They will inspire and help clarify how to prepare yours.

— EXAMPLE 3 —

Going to church was always a part of my life. The church I grew up in, however, was more focused on ceremony than teaching the Bible. I never understood I could have a relationship with Jesus myself or be sure of my salvation.

Then, a couple of things happened around the same time. First, I was talking with my husband's Aunt Viola, who comes from a similar background but, after studying the Bible, changed her viewpoint. She showed me that Christianity isn't about religious ceremonies but about developing a relationship with Jesus. She also explained that He alone offers assurance of salvation.

Around that time a friend mentioned a Christian music radio station. I started listening and enjoyed hearing people call in and talk about the assurance they have for their future. Finally, we started attending a new church where people worshiped God and also walked their faith daily. Everything fit together, what I'd heard from Aunt Viola, through the radio, and at church. It was at that time I dedicated my life to Christ.

My new relationship with Him gave me a strength I never had in the past. I am so grateful because about a year and a half ago, my father-in-law had a massive stroke that left him partially paralyzed. Throughout this trial, I've been able to rest on my faith and receive God's assurance as we support my in-laws. I know that He is in control and walking every step with us.

— EXAMPLE 4 —

When I was young, I was lucky enough to be raised in a Christian home and decided to follow Jesus at the age of nine. But all the way through to my college years, I lived to look good on the outside. I always had a smile on my face, said the right things, and stayed out of trouble. To my friends, teachers, and others, I was a good Christian kid. Yet my home life showed the real me. I fought with my sister, was disrespectful to my parents, and didn't care about anyone but myself. This closet ugliness continued into my marriage. I was kind to everyone I came in contact with, and then came home to "kick the dog" (a.k.a., my husband). After all, how could anyone expect me to be perfect all the time? It simply wasn't possible. I lived at war with myself. I was discouraged and knew I was a failure.

When I was about 25, I studied what the Bible said about life and especially about prayer. I saw how much God wanted to have a relationship with me.

He wanted to know me and for me to cling to Him and trust Him. God wanted my heart to know His heart. I realized that in everything I was doing *for* God, I didn't really *know* Him.

Now my life is different. I know that it is impossible to do anything good on my own because of my sin. Now I want to spend time with Jesus. I desire to know His heart and plan for my days. My outside is beginning to match my inside because God is at work in me.

Each of these stories show how a person raised in Christian circles can miss the essence of Christianity—knowing Jesus Christ. God used life situations to show each individual there was more.

Our Journey with Jesus stories and Converting stories will help create receptive insight and nudge people a bit closer to the God-saved life. They have a few things in common, I'll cover the similarities below. Once you learn these, you'll be able to craft your stories into meaningful gifts for others on a search for God. I call these the Dos and Don'ts of Your Stories.

— DOS AND DON'TS OF YOUR STORIES —

 300 Words or Less (about two minutes in length)

I suggest you divide your Converting stories into three segments: one-minute *before*, 45 seconds *how*, and 15 seconds *now*. Journey with Jesus stories have less of a framework, so I have no section recommendations. Just keep them short.

 Conversational and Nontheological Jargon

You must be ruthless at this point. You'll probably need a non-Christian or new Christian friend to listen and give you feedback as you craft and recraft your stories. They can tell you which words or thoughts you use that they don't understand. (I was just on the phone with my tax-preparer. I didn't understand a thing he was saying!) This happens all the time to curious or seeking people who want to understand but cannot because we are speaking Christianese. Another way to help you do this is to imagine you are telling your stories to the number-one person on your prayer list. That will help you craft it for their ears, not yours or your Christian friends.

Christ-Focused

Make sure Christ is the center of your stories. We're not talking about ourselves; we are talking about God's activity in our lives through Christ. We are not the heroes of our stories, Christ is.

 ### Identifiable Longing Within Your Story (for Converting stories, primarily)

Listeners will find commonality with you as you reveal real personal need that God awakened in you to help draw you to Himself. Look again at the point-in-time Converting stories. In the first, loneliness was my longing-cry. In the second, guilt was the longing-cry. In the two period-of-time Converting stories, we see a similar reality. In the first, the heart-cry was to know God personally. In the second, it was to find God and live a life focused on God and others rather than self. What was yours? Is that clear in your story? It should be. Go back to chapter 8, where I list the 12 human longings. Review them and consider your options. There could be more than one. If so, you have more than one story. All the better!

 ### Happily Ever After (*Not!*)

We are tempted to want to make our stories like Disney movies with a "happily ever after." But life is not that way. Even with Christ in us, we experience the sorrows and sufferings of life. Our stories should emphasize we are not alone any longer, that God is with us, makes us better, and walks with us in our challenges, but we still have challenges. (If you don't, please call me immediately because I want what you've got). Someday we will enter happily ever after, but that's another story, and it is literally out of this world.

Here are three examples of how to weave your Converting story into conversation with someone who is curious, or at least open. Each story is based on a true experience.

 ## TWO PASSENGERS ON AN AIRPLANE

Debby: *Hi, where are you heading today?*

Passenger: *I'm going to a funeral of a distant family member.*

Debby: *I'm sorry. Was it someone close to you?*

Passenger: *Yes, somewhat. (Conversation about the person and the connection ensues.)*

Debby: *It's so hard to face death. My husband and I just lost both his parents. Our faith in Jesus Christ has helped us face it. Do you have any spiritual beliefs to guide you in this time?*

Passenger: *I am Hindu.*

Debby: *I don't know much about Hinduism. What are some of the key beliefs in your faith, if you don't mind me asking?*

Passenger: *We have five principles and ten disciplines. I am not sure I can remember all of them, but I can give you the* *general idea if you are really interested?*

Debby: *Yes, I would like to hear them.*

Passenger: *Our five principles are that God exists in numerous divine forms, all human beings are divine, and unity of existence through love, religious harmony, and knowledge of the three Gs: Ganges river (for cleansing of sins), Gita (sacred script), and Gayatri (sacred mantras). Our ten disciplines are truth, nonviolence, celibacy or marital monogamy, no desire to possess or steal, noncorruption, cleanliness, contentment, reading of scriptures, regular prayers, and the practices of austerity, perseverance, and penance.*

Debby: *Those are fascinating. What do you do when you fail at keeping those disciplines? How do you receive forgiveness for your wrongs?*

Passenger: *We believe in karma. You will pay for what you have done wrong by receiving wrongs in your life.*

Debby: *Oh, I see. (Converting story) I made some bad choices in my life, and I definitely suffered some awful consequences. I was married with a family, but I was really sad and empty inside. I mistakenly thought that a divorce would bring me the happiness that I wanted, but it just hurt the people I love and made me hate myself. Fortunately, a caring friend took me to a Christian retreat. I heard the message of God coming to earth in the person of Jesus and dying on the Cross, paying the penalty for all the wrong I had done, and offering me forgiveness. That is what Christians call* grace, *or His overwhelming love. That message changed my life. I am no longer sad and empty* inside, and I no longer hate myself. Have you ever been interested in learning about the life of Jesus?

Passenger: *Actually, my children are going to a Christian preschool.*

Debby: *I bet one of the parents or pastors from the preschool would give you a Bible and tell you more about Jesus if you are interested.*

Passenger: *I may consider that. Thank you. And, thank you for sharing your story with me.*

Debby: *I promise to be praying for you and your family in your time of grieving.*

 TWO NEIGHBORS TALKING IN THEIR YARDS

Jim: *How are you doing?*

Neighbor: *I am exhausted—working a lot these days.*

Jim: *Sometimes, for me, it is not just the work, it's the stress and worry. Someone once shared a Bible verse with me that helps a lot. It says, "Do not be anxious about anything, but in every situation by prayer and petition, with thanksgiving, present your requests to God. And the peace of God, which transcends all understanding, will guard your hearts and your minds in Christ Jesus." Do you have any spiritual beliefs?*

Neighbor: *I went to church as a kid, but it was really boring. I don't believe too much in that heaven and hell stuff. I think we are all just supposed to do the best we can.*

Jim: *(Converting story) I went to church as a kid too. I was baptized and confirmed, but I never wanted to live a Christian life. To be honest, I wanted to run my own life and do what I wanted to do. But, even then, I felt something was wrong or missing in my life. All that changed when I thought I was going to lose my wife to Legionnaires' disease. I got down on my knees, and I gave my life over to Jesus. When you are facing the death of a loved one, being your own god doesn't work too well. My wife is now well, and I am so grateful. Having Jesus at the center of my life started changing everything. I am actually more fulfilled than ever, and I know when Linda and I die we will go to heaven, not because we have been perfect people but because we have received God's forgiveness for our wrongs. Would you ever like to discuss this a little more?*

Neighbor: *Yeah, that sounds interesting.*

Jim: *How about coffee on Saturday at 9:00 a.m.?*

 NEIGHBORHOOD PARTY

Jamie: *How do you know Tom and Kim (party hosts)?*

Sarah: *I went to college with Kim.*

Jamie: *It is great that you stayed connected.*

Sarah: *Do you know them because you live near?*

Jamie: *Yes, and also because I attend a Bible study with them in their home on Tuesday nights. It's very enjoyable and helpful. What do you like to do in your spare time?*

Sarah: *I like to ride my bike and garden. How about you?*

Jamie: *I enjoy bike riding and gardening as well. I also like the Bible study. I've actually started serving at a local church. I work in the nursery. I just love those little babies. What about you? Do you have any spiritual practices?*

Sarah: *No, I am not much into church. I don't really think much about it. I pray. I try to be good. I think I will go to heaven when I die.*

Jamie: *(Converting story) I never really thought about it much either. Though now that I look back on my life, I can see that something was missing. Then I hit a real crisis with my handicapped son. I felt alone, lost, and hopeless. In desperation, I picked up a book that a friend gave me. It was full of stories about how Jesus changed people's lives, giving them hope and direction. As I read the book, a lightbulb went off. I realized it might be Jesus that I was looking for in my life. A personal relationship with Jesus filled that empty place in my life. Now I know that no matter what I face He is with me. Sarah, would you be interested in reading about Jesus? If you'd like, we'd love to have you visit our Tuesday night group.*

Sarah: *Yes, maybe. I'm not much of a reader, but I would be interested in reading a book like the one your friend gave you.*

Jamie: *I have just the thing. It's a short book that explains the essential Christian message. Can I bring it over sometime this week, or do you want to drop by for coffee so I can give it to you?*

Sarah: *Sounds good.*

As you can see from these stories, being able to share your Converting story in everyday conversation is quite easy and natural. You can do this!

So far we've talked about how Share 1 is Their Story, the life of the listener. It's about learning to listen and ask questions to discern the stories of those we hope to influence for Christ. Share 2 is Our Stories—learning to know our own spiritual stories, both Journey with Jesus and Converting stories, and becoming skilled at telling them. They really are spiritual CPR. Now we move to Share 3: God's Story. We will learn to comprehend and communicate the greatest of all stories, the story of God's rescue of the world. And to make it personal, the rescue of those we love and long to see know Jesus Christ.

CHAPTER 10

Share 3
God's Story

NOT long ago, after Marie and I woke and sat together over morning coffee, we went about our personal devotions. My cell phone was sitting where I usually place it, face down, having charged overnight. Sometimes I look at it even before coffee and prayer, but not this day. I just left it there. Now, with devotions finished and before leaving for my office, I picked up the phone, turned it over, and saw a message on the screen. There it was. The best messages ever received: *At 7:14 this morning, Courtney [our daughter] gave birth to a beautiful, healthy baby girl.* Good news! Great news! No news could've been better. Our granddaughter had arrived. For us, it rivaled the shepherds at Christmas who received a great message from an angel, "I bring you good news that will cause great joy for all the people. Today in the town of David a Savior has been born to you; he is the Messiah, the Lord" (Luke 2:10–11). Good news!

THE COMING OF JESUS IS NOT MERELY A PHILOSOPHICAL IDEA TO BE DEBATED NOR A SET OF THEOLOGICAL PRINCIPLES TO BE OBEYED. IT IS THE STORY OF ALL STORIES—THE ULTIMATE GOOD STORY.

A grandchild is good news for family and friends. The birth of Jesus in Bethlehem is good news not for just one family but the human family of the world. The word *gospel*, which we see so often in the New Testament, means "good news." We need to start there and let that sink in. The coming of Jesus is not merely a philosophical idea to be debated nor a set of theological principles to be obeyed. It is the story of all stories—the ultimate Good Story. In fact, in the old English from which we derive the contemporary word *gospel*, it literally means "good spell" or "good story." A real, historical, nonfiction story. It is flesh and blood stuff brought to us by the Creator of the universe for every-one who exists. It is so good it must be shared—not just because God commands us to share it but because we are compelled to. We can't imagine keeping it to ourselves.

But there is some definition to this good news of God. It gives purpose to the One who came at Bethlehem. He will be a Sav-ior. *Savior? Who needs saving?* We do. I'm going to use a synonym for *Savior* because *Savior* is one of those words we Christians use so often it sometimes loses it vibrant impact. Even the best words become like a dull knife with overuse. I use the word *Rescuer* in its place. To need rescue means there is a crisis at hand, and usually the crisis is life threatening. The good news from the angel to the shepherds was the announcement of a massive human rescue in the making.

On August 5, 2010, a large mining operation at the San José mine in Chile went horribly bad. The mine collapsed 2,300 feet underground, trapped 33 miners, and instantly captured the attention of the world. The nation of Chile was in shock. Only six months earlier, they had suffered a large earthquake and tsunami. A global alert was sounded. Three major international drilling rig teams and more than a dozen multinational corporations from nearly every continent, including the National Aeronautics and Space Administration (NASA) from the United States, deployed with one purpose: rescue. Approximately $20 million in funds were used in the rescue, with nearly a third of that arriving through charitable contributions. Nearly every day the Chilean disaster and rescue operation was at the top of every news cycle. I remember watching the story 69 days after the disaster took place as 33 very sick and weary miners came out of the mine, all living, all alive, all rescued. The world rejoiced at such good news.

Similarly, the good news that we call the gospel is good news of a mighty rescue. God came down to rescue the world from two immense dangers. The first was the fast-spreading, ravaging disease of sin breaking and disordering everything and everyone. The second was to rescue all creation and creatures from an impending and imminent judgment on sin and sinners that a righteous and just God had every right to impose.

To express it another way—in approximately the year 5 BC, all the inhabitants and the earth were in cataclysmic danger. The disease of sin, a fast-spreading destruction of all that was good and beautiful, was making all things horrid, making what was perfect putrid. Further, the Creator and Authority over all things, which He'd made right and good, was bound by His own dictates to bring judgment against such devastation.

In an act of indescribable grace, God sent His Son to rescue His world to stop the devastation. Wherever the Son went, wrong was made right. He stopped the disease penetrating every mind and body and every created thing. He absorbed the disease and willingly took the judgment of death upon Himself. He was the only possible antidote. This was accomplished by means of a Roman cross in Jerusalem of Palestine in approximately the year 30 AD. The Bible repeatedly states He freed Himself from death three days later and lived in a resurrected body on earth with His people for 40 days, displaying complete power over all things, even the dimensions of space and time.

At the moment of His choosing, with many watching, He ascended to the skies and, by His own testimony, has now taken His place with God the Father as the authority over all things in heaven and on earth (Matthew 28:18). Before departing, He declared He would return, inaugurating a new heaven and earth where there shall never again be the disease of sin and where only righteousness and harmony exist in all things and creatures. The rescue will be final and complete for all who believe and follow Him. Only those who do not believe in Him and thereby reject the gift of His death in their place will be judged with the penalty of everlasting separation from Him and all that is good.

Until that time, His followers live on an earth where the control of sin has been broken in them. They are not perfect, but they are utterly changed for the good, with goodness growing in them. They carry His mandate to spread the good news, the story of rescue. Further, they are, by His Spirit's enabling power, mandated to make everything that is wrong right—as much as His will enables, wherever they dwell.

HIS FOLLOWERS LIVE ON AN EARTH WHERE THE CONTROL OF SIN HAS BEEN BROKEN IN THEM. THEY ARE NOT PERFECT, BUT THEY ARE UTTERLY CHANGED FOR THE GOOD, WITH GOODNESS GROWING IN THEM.

This is the good story (gospel) of God. To coin the title of a famous film about Jesus, it is the greatest story ever told. It is a story of historical events (life, death, Resurrection, ascension of Jesus Christ) and the promised results of those events, namely wisdom for living rightly, forgiveness of sin, the presence and power of God within every follower, and the promise of everlasting life with God and all who followed Jesus. These are enormous events and results benefiting humankind. This is the good news story of God's rescue.

Now comes the tricky part. We've been commissioned to tell others of these events and results and urge them to be rescued by becoming His followers. "We are therefore Christ's ambassadors, as though God were making his appeal through us" (2 Corinthians 5:20). "Go into all the world and preach the gospel to all creation" (Mark 16:15). It's pretty clear. It is also daunting and complex. Sometimes I hear Christians say, "Just speak the simple gospel." Well, it's not simple. It is a profound concept rivaling anything that philosophy or science can suggest to the world. But—and here is God's good promise—He will speak it through us. He will speak, and by His divine order, your words will have the power of God to bring understanding, conviction, and life reordering to the listeners. I promise to provide ways to tell this majestic good news story briefly and clearly, but before that, I'd like to share some stories of how God used people like you and me to perform His rescue. I hope these give us courage and energy as we fulfill our roles as ambassadors of the story.

— EXAMPLE 1 —
Marie Allison

It was a June morning. It was summertime and beautiful outside. The day before I had prayed to the Lord, "Now, Lord, it's been such a long time since I've seen someone come to know You. Could I please see someone come to know You?" So that next morning, when I was having my morning devotions, I took a piece of paper and reviewed the gospel, and I kind of pretended in my mind I was sharing it with someone who'd never heard it before. I diagrammed a bridge illustration [which I will teach later in this chapter]. When I'd finished I put my books and things down on the floor. At that very minute, the doorbell rang. If angels could sing and the heavens light up, it would have because I thought, *This is my spiritual appointment.* This is the person God wants me to share with today. I opened the door, and there was a young 20-year-old woman selling magazines.

They're trained to start off by sharing their life story, and she had had a very difficult life. Then she said, "I am out here going door to door selling magazines because I want to have a better life." How could I say no to that? So, we sat down on my cement step, and I bought a magazine from her. Then, because I had prayed that prayer the day before and because I had just practiced the gospel, I felt bold. I turned to her and said, "Has anyone every told you that you can have a relationship with God through Jesus Christ?" She said, "No." I said, "Would you like to hear that now?" She said, "Yes."

I grabbed copies of my *Steps to Peace with God* booklets, which are a go-to method for me. It was published by the Billy Graham organization and has been used to simply and clearly explain the essence of the gospel in a small booklet. I like it because it helps me to not forget anything if I'm nervous. I read through it with a person and then I give them the copy to take with them. It's always been well received. I had two copies of the booklet: one for me, one for her.

That way she could read her own without me being too much in her space as I read. I asked her to read the first two pages. She did. It's so good. It says God's purpose is peace and life and that God wants us to know such peace. Then it asks a great question. "Why don't most people have this peace and abundant life that God planned for us?"

That question really resonated with her. And she looked at me as if saying, "Yeah, why don't we?" We went through the whole booklet and at the end she asked the Lord into her life.

Before she left I said, "You know if you come back at the end of your shift, I will give you a Bible." She did! She came back at the end of her shift. I had collected several of our extra Bibles. Some were lightweight. One was a big study Bible. And I thought, *Oh, she's going to take the lightweight one because she is selling magazines, and they're staying in hotels and they're moving place to place.* But she went right for that big study Bible and she said, "You know I tried to read the Bible once before, and I couldn't understand it. So I think this one will help me." She walked away with it under her arm.

What a great story of being available to share the gospel by telling a receptive person, even a stranger, the story of Jesus, which as we said, includes the events and the results of His life. The gospel is a story with life-changing power. God called our friend on that day at that place to hear, believe, and receive Jesus Christ as Lord. Remember the words of the Apostle Paul in that regard? "I am not ashamed of the gospel, because it is the power of God that brings salvation to everyone who believes" (Romans 1:16).

— EXAMPLE 2 —

I was in Tel Aviv, Israel, with some church members on a mission. I'd been asked to speak at an international church that morning with about 100 people in attendance. Two Jewish believers and their wives led the service in English. The attendees, who were from six different continents, were primarily Christians. It was wonderful to worship with them and preach to them. On the day before the meeting, I'd decided on the text and sermon I would preach.

The more I prayed and thought about it, though, there was a disquiet in my soul. When the morning came, I changed the sermon and chose a second one I'd brought on the trip. It presented a stronger gospel message and called for attendees to receive Christ as Lord, should anyone be interested and called by God to do so.

After arriving at the church, I asked one of the Jewish leaders, my friend Dan, if he thought any nonbelievers would attend. He said, "Yes, probably." So, I preached. After getting about halfway through the sermon, I had a strong sense to let people know I would be offering an invitational prayer at the end of the message in case there was anyone who was unsure of their faith or who had not yet heard they could personally know God through Jesus Christ. I finished preaching and gave an invitation and said if anyone prayed the prayer with me to see me following the service. The service ended, and the congregation milled about in conversation when a young woman came up to me.

She looked a bit embarrassed, and English was clearly not her heart language. So I said, "Is there anything I can help you with?" She looked a bit surprised and said, "Well, you said that if anyone prayed the prayer with you, we should talk with you following?" I gulped a bit. "Yes, I did," I replied. "Did you pray that prayer to receive Christ as your Lord?" "Yes, I did." She had a big beautiful smile at this point. I talked with her about her decision and had every sense she was born again. I worried, though, as to whether she would have anyone to help her in her new-found faith. There are very few believers in Israel, and follow-up is a real concern. That's when she told me her sister would help. At this point the sister was smiling and standing next to her.

These sisters were Jewish. One of them had found Christ a few months earlier and was being discipled weekly by Dan's wife.

Undoubtedly, she'd been praying for her sister. On the Saturday morning of our service (Sunday is a workday in Israel, so worship occurs on Saturday), her sister said yes to an invitation to attend a Christian church. She had never been in a Christian church and had never heard the good news story in her life. But on that day, in that place, after one hearing, God drew her to Himself.

"Amazing love! How can it be that thou, my God should die for me?" The words of Charles Wesley's wonderful hymn come back to me now. The goodness of God and the persuasive power of His gospel story were at work in our midst.

— EXAMPLE 3 —
From a missionary friend in a
"Restricted Access" country

I was meeting with a new believer in the refugee camp. He had been listening to our radio station and became a believer after having a dream. The young man has four brothers. They persecuted this young believer in many difficult ways. We prayed for them, and slowly they became more open to listen. Eventually, three of them agreed to attend our meeting in the camp. All three of them gave their lives to Jesus. They have become strong believers and are living many experiences with Jesus. Three weeks ago I met the oldest brother, the one yet to convert. We all prayed for him, laying hands on him. That same day he saw Jesus in a wonderful dream.

The gospel moves with power through radio waves, dreams and visions, the faithful, and sometimes persecuted witness of family members. To God be the glory. I hope these examples have steeled your confidence in the gospel to rescue.

How do we tell people about the good news of God's rescue? There is so much to tell. The historical events of the gospel are comprehensive, and when we add the meaning or the results of those events, it is overwhelming. How could anyone understand all of it in one sitting? Does it all need to be told every time we share it? The gospel cannot usually be downloaded from one mind and mouth and understood by a listener in a few minutes. The brightest theological minds in the world spend lifetimes studying its depths. Why would we expect, apart from a divine miracle of understanding, that it can be understood and embraced so quickly?

My approach, therefore, is to offer a clear and concise summary of the gospel events and results. As an interested person responds, the larger truths within it can be shared through ongoing teaching. The gospel has the power to save or rescue even if the full weight and meaning of the gospel is not comprehended. Let me give an example. A few months ago my wife bought me a new tablet. I have been an Apple products aficionado, but this tablet was an Android with its own features and operating requirements. I hoped I would be able to quickly learn to navigate it and use it effectively. After charging it and turning it on, I found that I could do a small tutoring program to get its essential features explained. It also contained a larger explanation of everything about it. The small tutoring program, which I went through in just a few minutes, taught me enough to begin to experience the "riches" of the tablet. Several months later, I'm learning more and more about it and what it offers. The more I use it, the more I understand and the more it benefits me.

It's the same with the gospel. You don't need to feel you understand the depth of its riches before you share it with others. And, you don't need to feel you must explain all its riches before you share it. What needs to be shared is the central message of rescue. I recommend that you learn to share the essential details of the

IT'S THE SAME WITH THE GOSPEL. YOU DON'T NEED TO FEEL YOU UNDERSTAND THE DEPTH OF ITS RICHES BEFORE YOU SHARE IT WITH OTHERS. AND, YOU DON'T NEED TO FEEL YOU MUST EXPLAIN ALL ITS RICHES BEFORE YOU SHARE IT.

historical event that brought about the rescue and the results or benefits of the events. What are the essential details? The Apostle Paul helps us with this:

> *Now, brothers and sisters, I want to remind you of the gospel I preached to you, which you received and on which you have taken your stand. By this gospel you are saved . . . For what I received I passed on to you as of first importance:* that Christ died for our sins according to the Scriptures, that he was buried, that he was raised on the third day according to the Scriptures.
> —1 Corinthians 15:1–4 *(author's emphasis)*

He concludes this theme in the eleventh verse with an emphatic statement. "Whether, then, it is I or they [other apostles], this is what we preach, and this is what you believed." This is what we share. This is Paul's synopsis. These are the essentials, the historical events, and their results—Christ died and rose (events) to forgive our sins, to save us, and to lead us to belief (results). It is a great exercise to try to state the essential gospel in a sentence or two. Read the following examples, and see if both events and results of the rescue are intimated in each. I'll start with a couple of statements I use and then give you better ones from others:

Jesus died and rose to rescue sinners, including me.

God's loving actions rescued us, despite us.

I am so flawed that Jesus had to die for me, yet I am so loved and valued . . . Jesus was glad to die for me. —Tim Keller, *The Reason for God*

Christ died for us and rose again. —Larry Moyer, *Show Me How to Preach Evangelistic Sermons*

(For more examples, see the fine book by Mary Schaller and John Crilly, *The 9 Arts of Spiritual Conversations.*)

When we share God's story (good news) with someone, chances are we'll be able to say more than a sentence. We will need to. However, we don't need to give the depth of the whole thing either. What's important is to remember the two parts of the story: the events—His death and Resurrection—and the results—rescue and forgiveness of sins for those who receive Him.

How do we get to the point in a conversation when we share the most important news story in the universe? This takes us back to question asking. Generally you will know when it is time. The listener has moved from curiosity to seeking the truth about God and Christ. The listener will most likely be asking questions. They are deeply listening and pondering what you are saying, and you sense that receptivity because you are listening deeply to God while you are listening to them. In other words, someone ready to hear God's rescue story is more than curious, they are seeking it.

When I talk with people at this level, I get a sense that God is taking over the conversation guiding me to the right words and nudging the listener from curiosity to seeking or searching for more. If I've had the opportunity to share one of my Converting stories at some point in my interactions with the individual, it has prepared their heart and mind to want to know more and to experience something of what we've described. Sharing your story very often leads to an open door to share God's Story.

You might be wondering how we make the transition to sharing God's story. It is good to ask permission to share. Here are a few ways to do that:

"It seems you are interested in knowing God more deeply. Would you allow me about five minutes to explain the central message from the Bible about knowing God?"

"Are you interested in knowing God personally? If so, I can explain how in just a few minutes. May I?"

"May I take just a few minutes to explain why and how God loves you so much?"

"Have you begun a personal and meaningful relationship with God? If not, may I share how it can happen for you today?"

You can come up with even better questions, I'm sure. Each situation is a bit different, and the conversation preceding this point usually determines how you approach "the ask." When a seeking person responds yes to my offer of hearing God's story, it is truly joyous for me. I feel so privileged to be involved. So, what do we say? You've heard me say you don't have to share everything. But what *should* be said? What you say next is even more important than knowing your Journey with Jesus and Converting stories. This is God's story!

I believe every person can and should be ready to share the gospel message clearly, briefly, and in two ways. The first is from memory. The second is to use supporting material such as an app or tract. Let's look at a few methods you can use to share the gospel from memory.

GOOD NEWS, BAD NEWS, GREAT NEWS

Marie and I both like this method. It focuses on the deep need for a relational connection with the God who loves us. All humans long for loving relationships, and this model offers that through a relationship with God. It is also very clear and easy to remember. You see how it uses the Word of God, offering brief Scriptures to support the three types of news. The example I use below is as if I were sharing it with my neighbor Rick.

Good News: Rick, God's story begins with the good news that God created us and the world because He loves us deeply. The Bible says all over the place, "God is love" (1 John 4:16).

Bad News: However, there is bad news. Our wrong thoughts and behavior and our incessant focusing on ourselves at the expense of others separates us from Him because He is perfect and pure, and we are just so not. (Wrongful behavior includes the wrong things we think about, say, or do as well as the right things we don't think about, say, or do). The Bible teaches that, "There is no one righteous, not even one" (Romans 3:10) and, "Your iniquities have separated you from your God" (Isaiah 59:2).

Great News: Fortunately there is great news. The Bible says, "But God demonstrates his own love for us in this: While we were still sinners, Christ died for us" (Romans 5:8). Rick, what this means is that out of sheer love, Jesus, God's Son who was perfect and pure, took the penalty for all our wrongdoing on Himself so we could be restored to a right relationship with God.

Once you have shared the three points above, it is time for another question. I call it the decision question. For many of us, this is the hardest one to ask. Fear can grip us, and Satan tempts us to not do this. Sometimes we are afraid we didn't say the gospel well enough, so we don't ask the decision question. Other times we're afraid of getting a negative response. And our fear of the "no" is because we don't want to feel rejected or at least we're concerned the relationship will be a bit awkward from that point forward. I understand. I've lived with these fears for 46 years. They never go away. But I have gotten used to them. It helps me to remember that our God is a "calling" God. He is the one doing the inviting of this person. We are His ambassadors. When you and I ask the decision question, we are fulfilling the duties of ambassador, duties God gives us. Remember also, the conversion of the person is God's business and initiative, not ours. Ask the question. Leave the results with Him and the person.

Decision Question: Rick, would you like to live in a restored and loving relationship with God starting right now? The Bible says we can, "Everyone who calls on the name of the Lord will be saved [rescued]" (Romans 10:13).

If the person says yes, I recommend praying with the person at that moment. Since prayer is talking with God, it is the primary way to make the connection. I recommend a simple prayer I've borrowed from my colleagues who lead the Alpha Course movement, and which you can read about in their publication, *Questions of Life* by Nick Gumbel. Like Good News, Bad News, Great News, their prayer outline is simple to remember. It has four parts:

I am sorry (for my sin)

Please (forgive me)

Thank you (for Your Son/for forgiveness)

Please (come into my life)

We recommend you say the prayer in small segments and have them repeat it silently or out loud depending on the setting.

— EXAMPLE —
The Prayer of Commitment

Dear Lord,

I am sorry for the wrong things I think, say, and do.

Please forgive me. I want to turn away from them.

Thank You for sending Jesus to die for my sins and then rise from death. Thank You that because of that I can be forgiven for all my sins.

Please come into my life. I commit my life to follow You. Amen.

That is the Good News, Bad News, Great News model. You don't have to memorize it word for word, but do memorize the ideas or thoughts and put them in your own words. Try to memorize any Scripture you use word for word.

GOOD NEWS, BAD NEWS, GREAT NEWS—ILLUSTRATED

The second model I offer is Good News, Bad News, Great News but using what has been called the Bridge Illustration to explain it. You'll need a piece of paper—even a napkin will do— to draw it out.

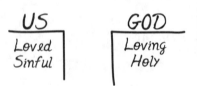

*The **GOOD NEWS** is that God loves us and created us to be in loving relationship with Him. The Bible says, "God is love" (1 John 4:16).*

*The **BAD NEWS** is that our sinful behavior separates us from a Holy God. Sin includes both the wrong things we do and the right things we don't do.*

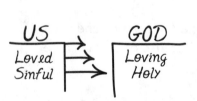

The chasm between us and God is too wide to jump over, but we are industrious people so we try to build our own bridge. But, however hard we try, however many good deeds we do, it is never enough to reach a Holy God. The gap is too wide. The Bible says, "There is no one righteous, not even one" (Romans 3:10), and, "Your iniquities have separated you from your God" (Isaiah 59:2).

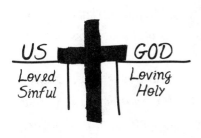

Fortunately, there is **GREAT NEWS.** The Bible says, "God demonstrates his own love for us in this: While we were still sinners, Christ died for us" (Romans 5:8). That means Jesus Christ paid the penalty for our sins so that we could be in a relationship with God.

Have you trusted in Christ to bridge the gap between you and God?

Would you like to do that now? (If they answer "yes," then lead them in prayer.) The Bible says, "Everyone who calls on the name of the Lord will be saved" (Romans 10:13).

Your words do not change, and the decision question and prayer do not change. But the illustration makes the meaning even clearer. And, you can then leave the drawing with the person whether or not they made a decision for Christ. That way they will have the memory of your conversation close at hand. If it is a stranger you are sharing this with, consider whether it is prudent to leave your email address (better than your phone number) for further contact should they desire. The offer of ongoing conversation is a gift of love and accentuates the "Care" you have for the person.

SICK, HURT, AND HEAL

Another model I use is Sick, Hurt, and Heal. This model relates sin to disease and hurt and relates the death and Resurrection of Jesus Christ to healing. Again, I will pretend I am talking with one of the people on my prayer list.

Annabel, I'm glad you want to know more about God and are making a place for Him in your life. I'm going to write out three

four-letter words to explain why this is so important: SICK,
HURT, and HEAL. Just as the body can get sick, so can our
souls. In fact, the Bible teaches that we all have a serious and
fatal soul sickness. Here are the symptoms of the sickness:

S=SENSUALITY—*People misuse and abuse the beautiful*
bodies God has given us. Some of us overindulge in what we
put into our bodies with uncontrolled appetites for food, drink,
drugs, etc. Some of us struggle to control our sexual appetites.

I=IDOLATRY—*Some of us make gods out of things that*
are not God. This can be people or things. It can often be good
things that we make bad because we make them into an idol.
Our work, our relationships, our families, and our wealth can
all become idols. As one writer has said, there are no atheists.
We all make gods out of something.

C=CONSUMPTION—*By this I don't mean the old nine-*
teenth-century disease. Rather, I mean the lust for things.
Sometimes things don't reach the level of gods (idolatry) but
wanting more and more things or wealth, which the Bible calls
greed, is another symptom of soul disease. The acquisition of
more things won't satisfy for long.

K=KILLING RELATIONSHIPS—*There are lots of ways*
we injure others with our thoughts, words, and actions. God
tells us to love others as we love ourselves, but often we hate
and hurt others or are victims of being hated or hurt by others.

This soul "SICK-ness" is what the Bible calls sin. "For everyone
has sinned; we all fall short of God's glorious standard" (Romans
3:23 NLT).

What is the prognosis for our soul SICK-ness, or sin? This leads to our next four-letter word, HURT, and our prognosis:

H=HEREDITARY—*Like certain physical diseases, the disease of sin is hereditary. We were actually born with the inclination toward sin.*

U=UNIVERSAL—*Sin sickness is universal. It's in every ethnicity and every generation. Even the most casual study of cultures all over the world suggests this is the case.*

R=REGRESSIVE—*Sin sickness never stays localized. It spreads. Like a fast spreading cancer, it grows to be an aspect of every part of our souls. We are getting sicker. Education doesn't cure it; government cannot slow it.*

T=TERMINAL—*The Bible says, "The wages of sin is death" (Romans 6:23). This speaks of a physical death and an eternal spiritual death in the sense that this soul sickness separates us from a pure and holy God forever.*

Unless . . . unless there is a cure? Can humankind—and can you and I—find a way to HEAL?

The answer is no and yes. No, we can't find a way to be healed. If we could, we would've a long time ago. However, though we cannot heal ourselves of soul sickness, God can, He wants to, and He has provided a way to HEAL, which He shares in His Word, "'He himself bore our sins' in his body on the cross, so that we might die to sins and live for righteousness; 'by his wounds you have been healed'" (1 Peter 2:24).

Annabel, God's love for you and for me is so great that He has done for us what we could not do. He absorbed our soul sickness and its consequences when He hung on the Cross 2,000 years ago. He died in our place, carrying our sin with Him. But three days later, He rose from death and lives with God forever. Just as He is alive, the Bible tells us we can be made alive, made new by believing in Him. Listen to this verse, "Praise the Lord, my soul ... who forgives all your sins and heals all your diseases, who redeems your life from the pit and crowns you with love and compassion" (Psalm 103:2–4).

Decision Question: *Annabel, would you like to place your life in the hands of God and let Him heal you of your soul sickness?*

Prayer: *I'm sorry, please, thank you, please (see p. 211).*

The three ways presented above to share the gospel, God's story, can be quite easily remembered. They are:

1   Good News, Bad News, Great News

2   Good News, Bad News, Great News—Illustrated

3   Sick, Hurt, Heal

There are many other ways and methods to share the gospel. Your pastor may have a way he most prefers. Other books on personal evangelism will provide more opportunities. However, I believe it is less important to be acquainted with many methods than it is to know one method well. Find one that you prefer, and practice, practice, practice until it becomes a part of your life. Imagine knowing God's Story as well as you know your own address. That's the goal. Consider these practicing tips.

Write out the method you want to use in your own words. Writing out what we learn helps better retain the information. Edit your first attempt, and then edit two more times. Each time you'll find ways to improve it. Each time it will go deeper into your memory bank.

Practice it with Christians. If you are in a small group, ask permission to do it with the whole group. As you meet with Christian friends, ask for five minutes to practice with them. Try to practice once a week for a month. Ask for critique each time, just as I encouraged you to do when crafting your stories.

Practice it with someone on your prayer list. That's right! Share it with someone who truly needs to be rescued from sin. I will never forget doing this with my mother when I was about 20 years old. I was the first in my household to embrace Christ. A couple of years after being rescued by God, I went to an evangelism seminar and learned how to use a tract to share God's story. The leaders said, on Friday night when the seminar began, that we had to share it with someone who needed to hear it before the weekend was over. So, I asked my mother if she would let me share it with her since it was my assignment. She gladly agreed, and at the end affirmed that while she thought she was a believer, she had not been a practicing believer for more than 20 years. I'd be lying to say that my sharing God's story with her that night made her become a fully devoted follower. It didn't, but it was a clear spiritual beginning of renewal for her. Over the next couple of years, my mother evolved into a lovely, devoted follower of Jesus. My sharing was simply one of the links in God's plan for her. So, practice with someone who needs it.

I promised to provide you two ways to share God's story. The first was to ask you to memorize a presentation. The second way is to use a small booklet or app. I used to hate tracts or gospel booklets. They seemed terribly impersonal. I've changed. There are several advantages to using an app on your smartphone or an attractive and appropriate printed booklet. I have both at my disposal. I haven't used the app yet, but I have colleagues who have and do.

What are the advantages of using printed materials or your device? First, the content they provide goes with your friend or acquaintance after you've finished your time together. In the case of an app, they can always download it on their own device. They can refer to it later and review what you shared. Second, it is nice to have the words in a printed format in case you forget what to say. Third, the printed formats have excellent graphics that assist in "filling out the meaning" of the words. Fourth, in our world of increasing ethnic diversity, we may be sharing with someone for whom English is not their heart language. Both the tracts I recommend can be purchased in other languages. Even if you only have an English booklet with you, you can readily help them find it in their own language on the web. Finally, sometimes you won't have time to adequately share God's story. Often in taxis going to the airport, I can do Share 1 and 2 but not get to Share 3—God's story. I've given interested passengers or drivers a booklet of God's story for their own perusal when they have more time.

I recommend the *Knowing God Personally* booklet, a relational rendering of the old *4 Spiritual Laws* created by Bill Bright and the Cru organization. I also recommend the app version of *Knowing God Personally*, which you can find in the app store by searching *God tools app*. You can download it for free to your smart-phone or tablet. The person you're sharing with can download it after you share or while you are together so you can read together on your individual devices. It also has some nice follow-up features.

Our church also uses the booklet, *Steps to Peace with God*, published by the Billy Graham Evangelistic Association. It, like *Knowing God Personally*, has been used for decades. Both of those booklets have been used by God to bring countless thousands and perhaps millions to Christ. I was with a man using *Knowing God Personally* in downtown Nazareth, Israel, recently. His booklet was in Arabic. I saw this Arab brother lead two people to spiritual decisions in Nazareth and then make plans to meet again with them to help them understand the decision they made. How wonderful!

When using an app or booklet, here are a few tips:

1. **Give the listener their own booklet, or have them download the app before you share.** This allows the person to "have their own space" as they are reading the words. Western people don't like being too close to each other. Having their own device or booklet allows them to be more at ease.

2. **Stick with what is written.** Don't add too much to what is on the pages, or the person may get confused.

3. **Don't skip the decision question.** It's on the app or in the booklet. Don't fall for the temptation to not ask if they'd like to commit to Jesus. They may be far more ready than you think!

If you feel it's appropriate and you are using a booklet, give them your email if they'd like further contact.

Sharing God's rescue story is the most wonderful privilege in the world. May God provide many chances for you to do so starting now and for the rest of your life or until He returns.

We have now completed our journey of the three actions—Prayer, Care, and Share-Share-Share. I hope you are enjoying the ride so far. I certainly am. Now we turn course a bit to talk about the two essential attitudes necessary for a life of fulfilling and effective Witness-Life. They are Dare and Hanging in There—better known as courage and perseverance. As you'll see, these attitudes and actions combine beautifully to graciously point others to God.

CHAPTER 11

Dare to Share:
Courage

MARIE walked in the door after work a few days ago and said, "My ladies are afraid."

"Afraid of what?" I asked.

She has been teaching a small group of women, all new believers in Jesus, about Witness-Life and Prayer, Care, Share.

"Well, today I emphasized that now that we know how to share our faith, it is time to do it. Now they are afraid."

"Oh," I responded and then added, "I'm not surprised."

I'm not surprised for two reasons. The first may surprise you. I'm not surprised because I still fight against fear of witnessing. I've been doing it for about 46 years, and I'm still afraid. I've been trained to do it, and I'm still afraid. I've been gifted to do it, and I'm still afraid. I get paid to do it, and I'm still afraid. The second reason is because after 46 years of helping other Christians witness, the number one, two, three, four, five . . . reasons that hinder witness have fear at the base. Why are we not confident, why are we not courageous, why are we not daring?

It really is the "elephant in the room." All that we've learned about the Witness-Life, both the theology and the practical application skills, won't change much of anything in our lives

> STILL FIGHT AGAINST FEAR OF WITNESSING. I'VE BEEN DOING IT FOR ABOUT 46 YEARS, AND I'M STILL AFRAID. I'VE BEEN TRAINED TO DO IT, AND I'M STILL AFRAID. I'VE BEEN GIFTED TO DO IT, AND I'M STILL AFRAID. I GET PAID TO DO IT, AND I'M STILL AFRAID.

unless we figure out how to beat back fear and replace it with courage and daring. I am sure we can, so let's discuss it.

What are the causes of fear that so easily slow or cripple our Witness-Life?

FEAR OF PERSECUTION

Not long ago, I returned from a country in the Middle East where there are few Christians, and to admit to being a Christian can be dangerous. We received word recently from that area, a precious woman and her child were beaten on the way to their house church meeting. When I first met this woman, not long after her conversion to Christ, she and her husband welcomed us warmly and quietly into their home. Quietly? Yes. They closed the windows and drew the shades. We sat on the floor together because they are refugees from Syria and have few furnishings. Yet they were aglow with love for Jesus. They found Christ, or better, Christ found them through their struggle of escape and the loss of home and business. They also shared how Jesus miraculously healed the woman of a disease. They were careful about sharing their faith with others openly. The recent beating explains why. It would raise fear in anyone.

Such persecution is rare where we live. Yet we may experience a lighter version. Marie and one of her friends have drifted away from one another, in part because of Marie's faith in Jesus. When Marie shared her Converting story with her friend one day in a gentle and loving way, something in the relationship got a bit uncomfortable. Marie didn't push the woman to believe, she just shared her story. They are still on speaking terms, but it was never quite the same afterwards. There is no meanness or overt rejection. It is just that

Marie's faith is the centerpiece of her life, and it is not for the other person. So, there is a natural drifting. That can happen, but it doesn't very often. I can't remember it ever happening in my life. We live in a country that pretty much allows people to believe what they want as long as they don't hurt someone or become overly obnoxious because of it.

Still, I can't promise you it won't ever occur. Many colleagues argue that persecution will get worse, even in the United States. I don't know if that is correct. I've been hearing that for 40 years, and it seems to me it's still acceptable to have personal faith in Christ in most places in our country. What I can say for sure, however, is that our Lord Jesus experienced persecution too. He experienced rejection even from His own family (Mark 3:20–21). He was beaten and killed on the Cross for His faith. So, He understands the kind of rejection we may feel, and He experienced the physical abuse and rejection that our sister and her daughter experienced in the Middle East. He has prepared us for our persecution at whatever level we experience it. "Remember what I told you: 'A servant is not greater than his master.' If they persecuted me, they will persecute you also" (John 15:20).

I'd rather be shunned for my love for God than to hide my faith and hurt the heart of my Lord. I'd rather be shunned a bit than not love my neighbors and friends by keeping my faith a private thing. I mean, after all, how much do I have to not care for a person to keep the message of forgiveness of sins and eternal life a secret? I read a bold—but I believe helpful—quote this week from pastor and author David Platt, who said, "Every saved person this side of heaven owes the gospel to every unsaved person this side of hell." That works for me. We have to find ways to overcome our fear of persecution, and we will.

FEAR OF IGNORANCE

Often we fear that if we share our faith with someone, they will ask questions we don't know how to answer. If that happens, it is great! (I'm not being flippant.) It is great for at least three reasons. First, it means the person is at least interested and maybe even curious. I'll take that attitude any day over someone who has no interest. Second, it gives us a reason to go and find the answer. That takes us deeper into prayer and Bible study. That is a good thing. And finally, it almost guarantees you can have another opportunity to be in spiritual conversation with that person when you have found the answers, unless they were just arguing for argument's sake.

Let me teach you how to answer when someone asks a question you can't answer. You respond with seven words: "I don't know, but I'll find out." By the way, at the end of this book, I'll give some brief answers to the most commonly asked questions. That can get you started in finding answers.

FEAR OF BEING LABELED "ONE OF THOSE CHRISTIANS/EVANGELICALS"

We kind of get a raw deal in our culture. Media often lumps all Christians into the same pile of awful people who bomb abortion clinics, hate gay people, and always vote for mean-spirited, uncivil candidates for office. So, I agree we start with a couple of strikes against us.

I still remember a neighbor who became one of my best friends. When we met, I was careful not to go deep into my faith because he had voiced some of the views suggested above about

Christians. I didn't tell him I was an "evangelist," which to him would've been like saying I was an IRS agent. But within a couple of months of being together, I was able to tell him how much my faith meant to me and that I was an evangelist! You know what he said? He said, "I'm glad you didn't tell me right away. I'm glad I got to know you better first."

He remains a dear friend. And, though he was angry at God because of the loss of his father at an early age and skeptical because of his personality type and training in science, he is now a devoted follower and lover of Jesus. I actually embrace the challenge of having to break the stereotype of Christians by being a real one! Real Christians filled with the Spirit are full of love, joy, peace, patience, kindness, goodness, faithfulness, gentleness, and self-control (Galatians 5:22–23). Generally, others end up liking people like you and me when we are filled with God! We are to let our light shine for all to see.

> I ACTUALLY EMBRACE THE CHALLENGE OF HAVING TO BREAK THE STEREOTYPE OF CHRISTIANS BY BEING A REAL ONE!

FEAR OF BEING LABELED A SALESMAN

First of all, I know a lot of wonderful salespeople. I bet you do as well. What makes them wonderful at their work is believing in their products and how that product can benefit the potential client. They also have respect for the client and avoid manipulation for their own gain. Paul says it best. "Unlike so many, we do not peddle the word of God for profit. On the contrary, in Christ we speak before God with sincerity, as those sent from God" (2 Corinthians 2:17).

As I sit in our living room, I can look out a beautiful picture window and see a spring rain falling. The yard is freshly mowed, and the trees are blooming and greening in splendor. We love our home and are so grateful to God for it. My mind turns to the memory of Steve Randolph, the realtor who sold it to us. I'm very grateful he was assertive enough to search for and find this home. I'm grateful he spent time with us learning our needs and hopes for a home. I'm glad he was honest enough to dare to offend us when another house we might've wanted was out of our price range, and he told us so. I'm grateful he answered all our questions about every home we visited and was patient as long as we needed him to be before we bought this one. I like godly sales people like Steve. How much more those who care enough to share Christ, who answer questions, listen to doubts, give more information as needed, who are patient, and then who rejoice like the angels when any person turns to God.

FEAR OF NOT ENOUGH TIME

A student once voiced this fear to me, "If I share my faith in Jesus and a person responds and receives Him, then I have to disciple the person, and I just don't have the time. I have so much to do in life. I wouldn't know how to add it." That's a fair fear. I get it. I struggle with the same temptation. On the contrary, Jesus said, "But seek first his kingdom and his righteousness, and all these things will be given to you as well" (Matthew 6:33). The God who is beyond all time orders our time when we walk close to Him and seek His purposes.

I remember leading a young man named Terry to Christ. I wanted to help him grow but felt I was already too busy with family and work to do it. By faith and hope that God would help me with life management, I set up weekly breakfasts with him for a couple of months. You know what? I got the rest of my work done with no problem. And because of my time with the young man, I enjoyed life more. He reminded me of what it is to be fresh and young in faith. He asked the questions I'd long forgotten about and expressed a young and vibrant love for God and His Word that I, in my busyness, often lost. I was blessed richly by God and Terry.

And also, remember that God has lots of believers who want to help us disciple new believers. God has all the time in the world, and He uses all of us not only to reach people but help them grow. Our churches are longing for such opportunities, and other brothers and sisters would love to come alongside the Terry's of our lives.

THE BIG REASON FOR FEAR

Perhaps you have fears in addition to the ones I've addressed. But there is a bigger issue. None of these fear-fostering issues—and any others we can imagine—warrant the degree of fear we feel about them. It's almost as if the fear in these issues takes on a life of its own and gets bigger than the issues warrant. I wondered about this for a long time.

My personal breakthrough in the problem of fear was when I realized this in my own life. Once I objectively examined the issues contributing to my fears, I was surprised the fear was so great. After all, I've been at this for 46 years. No one has killed me yet. And rejection has been manageable, even beneficial. I've heard every question and have an earned doctorate in this field.

Why would questions scare me? I have seen the value of being stereotyped for my faith because I can display Christ and watch the stereotypes crumble. I categorically reject being called a selfish Jesus salesman because I love the people I share with and want their best. I don't get a bonus for sharing. It doesn't benefit me to lead someone to Jesus, though it sure feels good. Witness-Life is not about me. And though I'm busy, God has always ordered my time to have more than enough to care for young believers. Yet emotionally, the fears never recede. My fears were and are bigger than they should be when I look at the causes of them. Why is this so? I believe that behind every fear concerning the Witness-Life is the tempter and our adversary, the devil.

Part of the tempter's plot is to make things bigger than what they are in order to move us to sin and be less effective for Jesus on this earth. Sometimes the temptations feel like temporary insanity. If I'm tempted to greed, bitterness, or lust, those inclinations get turbocharged by the enemy of our souls. They move from being mere afflictions to near addictions! Fear of witnessing is also a temptation from hell. It may be more destructive in the end than the temptation to greed or bitterness or lust if it stops or even slows us from being the glad messengers of God's story. If God's ambassadors (you and me) can be thwarted in the Witness-Life by succumbing to tempting fears, it slows God's redemptive work on the earth. Therefore, this temptation must be dealt with like any other temptation from hell.

Fear is everywhere. "Fear not" is one of the most often repeated commands in the Bible. One writer says the command to "fear not" is used hundreds times in the Bible! And so, dear readers, let that command reach you as you consider your Witness-Life. Fear not.

God is serious about this. So serious, in fact, that while we are not to fall to Satanic-inspired fear, we should appropriately fear God, who has commanded and compelled us to share our faith. I don't mean fear in the sense of being punished for not witnessing, but rather, fear in the sense of having awesome respect for His will in this matter. I want to witness because it pleases Him, and He, who is my Lord, has commanded it. I bow and obey my living God. Let's look at some Scriptures. The first passage comes from the lips of our Lord concerning our Witness-Lives:

> *I tell you, whoever publicly acknowledges me before others, the Son of Man will also acknowledge before the angels of God. But whoever disowns me before others will be disowned before the angels of God.*
> —Luke 12:8–9

That is an eye-opening passage. Read it a couple of times. If you are like me, it leads to prayer and confession of how often I don't publicly acknowledge Him. I pray that He will enable me to do so consistently and winsomely. I want to please my Lord, not embarrass Him. Paul says, "We make it our goal to please to him" (2 Corinthians 5:9). I want to please Him because I love Him. When a congregant calls or texts to thank me for a word or sermon or prayer I offered on their behalf, I feel so grateful. I'm glad I've

I WANT TO WITNESS BECAUSE IT PLEASES HIM, AND HE, WHO IS MY LORD, HAS COMMANDED IT. I BOW AND OBEY MY LIVING GOD.

helped because I love them. How much more with our precious Lord? Now, carefully read the following passage where we're called to stand strong and go public with our faith regardless of consequences that launch our fears:

> *Think back on those early days when you first learned about Christ. Remember how you remained faithful even though it meant terrible suffering. Sometimes you were exposed to public ridicule and were beaten, and sometimes you helped others who were suffering the same things. You suffered along with those who were thrown into jail, and when all you owned was taken from you, you accepted it with joy. You knew there were better things waiting for you that will last forever. So do not throw away this confident trust in the Lord. Remember the great reward it brings you! Patient endurance is what you need now, so that you will continue to do God's will. Then you will receive all that he has promised.*
> —Hebrews 10:32–36 NLT

How do we overcome the temptation inflaming our fears keeping us from the Witness-Life? Since Satan is the author of temptation, we must address it the way we would other devil-driven temptations. Both James and Peter give us guidance in this area.

> *Submit yourselves, then, to God. Resist the devil, and he will flee from you. Come near to God and he will come near to you.*
> —James 4:7–8

> *Be alert and of sober mind. Your enemy the devil prowls around like a roaring lion looking for someone to devour. Resist him, standing firm in the faith . . . And the God of all grace, who called you to his eternal glory in Christ, after you have suffered a little while, will himself restore you and make you strong, firm and steadfast.*
> —1 Peter 5:8–10

As Peter says, first we should *be alert and sober* about this danger. That is why I'm drawing attention to this issue. We are in a supernatural battle against forces of darkness whose end goal is to cripple God's saving work and increase the population of hell. Be aware. Fear of witness is an enemy tactic. Second, *submit to God and draw near to Him.* Christians cannot defeat supernatural evil. Only God can. So our apostolic brothers rightly tell us to draw near to God. Hide in the shelter of His mighty arms. The battle is not ours but God's. I often cry out to Him with words like, "I can't beat this temptation, God. You can. Take it, Lord."

The third injunction in our passages is to *resist.* If you are alert to the attack and have submitted and drawn near to God, then resist the mental assault until God's relief comes. It will come. He always comes. Remember this text:

> *No temptation has overtaken you except what is common to mankind. And God is faithful; he will not let you be tempted beyond what you can bear. But when you are tempted, he will also provide a way out so that you can endure it.*
> —1 Corinthians 10:13

Finally, we are to *stand firm in faith*. Take up your shield of faith (Ephesians 6:16). Faith is trust and strong belief in God and His promises. Acts 4 details a magnificent story of God's people standing firm in faith concerning their witness and the fear they felt. In its early days, the young church enjoyed immense popularity in Jerusalem. That all ends by Acts 4. Peter and John are arrested and put in jail. The religious leaders, opposed to the new faith in Jesus, threatened them and the church repeatedly. They were to cease and desist. They were not to speak or teach at all in the name of Jesus (v. 18). They weren't told to deny their faith, but they were told to not speak about it with anyone. What follows is more than inspiring.

FAITH IS TRUST AND STRONG BELIEF IN GOD AND HIS PROMISES.

With fear rising in them, they submitted and drew near to God. They stood strong in faith, claiming God's sovereignty over all things, including this danger. Please read the report of their prayer meeting (vv. 24–28); it is loaded with faith and daring in the midst of fear. Fear was resident in them, but they overcame it with faith. Fear doesn't disappear and, at least in my life, never stops attacking. But faith resists fear and awaits God's deliverance.

Fear is constantly present in my Witness-Life. It hasn't gone away, but for the most part, I've gotten used to it. It crashes in every time I share God's Story, whether with one person or a thousand. But faith is the shield against fear's power. I believe God's Word about His story and sometimes with little more than sheer determination speak it. That is faith. I praise my God for granting me the faith to stand against the fear.

In verse 29, we see the final words of their prayers of faith.

"Enable your servants to speak your word with great boldness." They ask for boldness and daring greater than their fear. They get it! "After they prayed, the place where they were meeting was shaken. And they were all filled with the Holy Spirit and spoke the word of God boldly" (v. 31). Faith brings the presence and power of God, and they don't shrink back. Boldness filled them, and they acted on it. They obeyed their Lord to speak His good news and tell His story. Some of them will die for it. It didn't matter. As the great spiritual song, "The Battle Hymn of the Republic," says, "His truth is marching on." The same is true in our era of the human story. We dare to share.

FAITH IS THE SHIELD AGAINST FEAR'S POWER.

Let's quickly review the instructions and the Scripture we've received to help us dare to share:

1. Be alert.

2. Submit and draw near to God.

3. Resist.

4. Stand firm in faith.

CHAPTER 12

Hanging in There:
Perseverance

"NEVER give in, never give in, never, never, never, never—in nothing, great or small, large or petty—never give in." (Winston Churchill at Harrow School, 1941).

This quote from the prime minister of Great Britain during World War II has inspired me for decades. The context for his remarks was a massive war, and they were losing, badly. His army was being beaten on every front. But in this speech and others, he promised to never give up. He called the citizens of the British Empire not to quit either. They didn't, and in one of the most remarkable turnaround events of any century, the monstrous Nazi army was defeated.

This is the kind of tenacity we need to give us daily strength in our Witness-Life. Am I being melodramatic? No. This is serious. We are in the battle for souls. This battle is being fought in the world we see all around us and in the supernatural world we can't see.

A text just buzzed my phone. It is from a colleague at his mother's bedside. She has not yet surrendered her life to Christ. He and his siblings have prayed for her for decades. His church is praying for her now. We will not quit. I texted back two words: *praying now.*

Now my mind moves to our neighborhood. We cohost our neighborhood party in four days, and I'm too busy. My time is too crowded to spend it with a couple of the neighborhood men showing little openness to spiritual matters. I'm too focused on writing my book on witnessing to be praying every day for every neighbor to attend the party. We've been at this in our neighborhood for ten years. I'm ready to forget about the whole thing.

Wrong, wrong, wrong. Never give in. Never give in.

Anyone else like me?

Steve and Laura sent a note from California. Steve's dad, who died at 92, had lived a long life. I remember Steve's dad all the way back to January of 1978. Why? Because that's when Steve, Laura, Marie, and I started a church for unchurched people. Our parents all came to support us. Steve's dad was there on opening Sunday, but he seldom came after that. He didn't know Christ. He showed no interest in spiritual things. Five years later he still showed no interest. Ten years, 20 years, 30 years, 38 years—not interested. His wife, Steve's mother, came to faith. Two of the man's children entered God's family and his grandchildren as well, but not Mr. Chellew. Steve wept over his dad's spiritual condition. He prayed. He had others pray. He shared with his dad when he was open to it. Nothing for 38 years.

Then the word came. Old age was taking its toll. He was spiraling downward. A few days later, the surprise of joy. He had listened, finally, to the appeal of his Christian granddaughter and embraced the God who loved him from the foundation of time. God never quit on him. Then on Saturday he died, or better, he really started living. I can see his face in my mind in his early 50s stepping into our church to support his son in 1978. I saw him in his 60s, and I think even in his 80s. I won't see Mr. Chellew again until I meet him in the forever land. Never give in, never give in.

When I was a younger believer in my 20s, I couldn't imagine persevering in Prayer, Care, and Share, for more than 30 years for a man to come to Christ, but then I read the biography of George Müller. The great nineteenth-century believer is best known for founding orphanages in England. He had steel-strong persevering faith and is remembered for the way he trusted God for the funding to run his ministry. His biography tells story after story of God meeting every food and funding need for his children in the orphanages. But he also prayed for his friends without Christ.

> *He was an unwearied intercessor. No delay discouraged him . . . On his prayer list were the names of some for whom he had besought God daily, by name, for one, two, three, four, six, ten years before the answer was given. The year just before his death, he told the writer of two parties for whose reconciliation to God he had prayed, day by day, for over sixty years, and who had not as yet to his knowledge turned unto God: and he significantly added, "I have not a doubt that I shall meet them both in heaven" . . . It is most helpful here to add that one of the parties for whom for so many years he unceasingly prayed has recently died in faith, having receive the promises and embraced them and confessed Jesus as his Lord.*
> —*George Müller of Bristol* by Arthur T. Pierson

The story continues. The second of the two unconverted became a Christian shortly after Müller died. Whether it is faith that prays for something needed within the hour or faith to prevail in prayer for a lifetime, Müller's testimony points us to the God who is faithful to answer the prayers of His people and their persevering witness.

When I think of Mr. Müller or our friends Steve and Laura, I'm reminded of the verse, "Let us not become weary in doing good, for at the proper time we will reap a harvest if we do not give up" (Galatians 6:9). The text is calling for Christians to live noble and faithful lives as God would lead, and never give up in serving Him. Surely the living of a noble and faithful Christian life includes our Witness-Life?

PART OF THE HARDSHIP OF WAITING AND PERSEVERING IS THE PAIN. WHEN YOU LOVE DEEPLY YOU HURT HARD.

Part of the hardship of waiting and persevering is the pain. When you love deeply you hurt hard. We've already spoken about the mystery of God, how He draws our hearts toward the lost as He draws the lost toward Him. Sometimes I wish that wasn't so. Sometimes I'd rather not feel so deeply for those I love that are far from God. But it's part of the deal. The love of Christ compels us and as Paul wrote, causes some people to think we are crazy (2 Corinthians 5:13–14).

Pastor and author Francis Chan had it right when he named one his books, *Crazy Love*. That's what it is. It's crazy to care so much, at least if you look at it from the world's perspective. But there is no way around it. Our Lord wept over Jerusalem because her people would not receive Him (Luke 19:41). He could see that the price for rejecting Him would be the destruction of the city and its people. Earlier He said:

> *Jerusalem, Jerusalem, you who kill the prophets and stone those sent to you, how often I have longed to gather your children together, as a hen gathers her chicks under her wings, and you were not willing. Look, your house is left to you desolate.*
>
> — Luke 13:34–35

Since it is His love in us that yearns for others to know Him, then we can expect sorrows and tears like our Lord. It can be tempting to become callous or resigned. It is tempting to give up. It's tempting to distort our theology and begin to see people's rejection of God as part of an omniscient, sovereign will, and just give up. But it sure seems to me that Jesus' tears and sorrows when He was rejected were real as He longed for all to be saved. He hurt. We will too. But He never gave up. We won't either.

Just as we may have to persevere for long periods of time, so too we persevere through the pain of seeing people reject Him. When I'm tempted to resign in my calling to witness, I like to claim a text from one of the Psalms of Ascent. In this psalm, the writer remembers the long endurance of God's people—more than 70 years—waiting for God to bring His people home after captivity in foreign

IT SURE SEEMS TO ME THAT JESUS' TEARS AND SORROWS WHEN HE WAS REJECTED WERE REAL AS HE LONGED FOR ALL TO BE SAVED. HE HURT. WE WILL TOO. BUT HE NEVER GAVE UP. WE WON'T EITHER.

lands saying, "Those who sow with tears will reap with songs of joy. Those who go out weeping, carrying seed to sow, will return with songs of joy, carrying sheaves with them" (Psalm 126:5–6). I offer this text to any readers who, like us, still lament over those who say no or just don't seem to care about Jesus.

Like you, Marie and I have loved ones with whom we've prayed, cared, and shared with for decades, and we still wait. Hold on, brothers and sisters. Persevere. The psalm promises we shall someday sing songs of joy and carry the harvest of rescued lives with us to eternity. May it be so for your children and ours, your parents and ours. May it be so for your neighbors, your friends, your co-workers, and ours. I hear Churchill's words in my mind again, "never give in, never give in, never, never, never, never." We must take up our weapons of faith and our actions of prayer, care, and share until Christ returns or calls us home.

I'd like to end this section with a portion of an old poem I often read at the end of witness training conferences. It reminds all believers of our role of witness and goal of rescue for which we persevere. Since the poem was written more than 50 years ago, please excuse the use of the word "men" instead of "men and women" or "people." The use of "men" to represent all persons was common in that era.

> *I stand by the door.*
> *I neither go too far in, nor stay too far out,*
> *The door is the most important door in the world—*
> *It is the door through which men walk when they find God.*
> *There's no use my going way inside, and staying there,*
> *When so many are still outside and they, as much as I,*

Crave to know where the door is.
And all that so many ever find,
Is only the wall where a door ought to be.
They creep along the wall like blind men,
With outstretched, groping hands.
Feeling for a door, knowing there must be a door,
Yet they never find it . . .
So I stand by the door.

The most tremendous thing in the world,
Is for men to find that door—the door to God.
The most important thing any man can do,
Is to take hold of one of those blind, groping hands,
And put it on the latch—the latch that only clicks,
And opens to the man's own touch.
Men die outside that door, as starving beggars die,
On cold nights in cruel cities in the dead of winter—
Die for want of what is within their grasp.
They live, on the other side of it—live because they have not found it,
Nothing else matters compared to helping them find it,
And open it, and walk in, and find Him . . .
So I stand by the door.

. . . .

As for me, I shall take my old accustomed place,

Near enough to God to hear him, and know he is there,

But not so far from men as not to hear them,

And remember they are there, too.

Where? Outside the door—

Thousands of them, millions of them.

But—more important for me—

One of them, two of them, ten of them,

Whose hands I am intended to put on the latch.

So I shall stand by the door and wait,

For those who seek it.

"I had rather be a door-keeper . . ."

So, I stand by the door.

—"I Stand by the Door" by Samuel Moor Shoemaker

CHAPTER 13

Prepare Others

I SINCERELY trust that your confidence and hope are rising with the belief that God wants you to join Him in bringing people toward and to Jesus Christ. The joy that accompanies the journey makes up for the disappointments that are also part of it. You can do this. You were made for it. God is with you in the Witness-Life. We are almost done with the book but only beginning to live this kind of life. There is one more principle I'd like to share before we conclude. I have saved the best for last.

Let's wrap up by thinking about the joy of helping new and existing disciples catch the vision of the Prayer, Care, Share life. We use a term around our church that seeks to capture this joy and passion. We call it being 3-D people. We want to be 3-D people who are disciples, who make disciples, who make disciples. The idea is certainly not new to us. It emanates from Paul's mentoring instructions to his young protégé, Timothy. He wrote, "And the things you have heard me say in the presence of many witnesses entrust to reliable people who will also be qualified to teach others" (2 Timothy 2:2).

YOU CAN DO THIS. YOU WERE MADE FOR IT. GOD IS WITH YOU IN THE WITNESS-LIFE.

Imagine the unstoppable movement of the gospel if those who live a Witness-Life would train and inspire other new and existing believers to join them in its practice and that they would give the same gift to others. A cycle like that would never end. It would rapidly accelerate the flow of God's rescue story throughout the earth. This is probably what happened in the early centuries of the church.

Rodney Stark, in his book, *The Rise of Christianity*, wrote of the phenomenal growth of early Christianity. He suggests that at the end of the first century, there were more than 7,000 believers. That means that in about 70 years the church, which began circa 30 AD in that Jerusalem upper room on Pentecost with 120 believers, spread to more than 7,000 souls. We know from the Book of Acts that they were scattered in many parts of the Roman Empire. Stark believes that by the end of the fourth century, God's people had grown to more than 33 million persons, nearly half of the Roman world. That could only have happened by multiplication. Disciples made disciples who made disciples.

IMAGINE THE UNSTOPPABLE MOVEMENT OF THE GOSPEL IF THOSE WHO LIVE A WITNESS-LIFE WOULD TRAIN AND INSPIRE OTHER NEW AND EXISTING BELIEVERS TO JOIN THEM IN ITS PRACTICE AND THAT THEY WOULD GIVE THE SAME GIFT TO OTHERS.

Not long after I became a Christian, someone taught me about God's desire for His people to multiply throughout the world. The teacher made a distinction between adding and multiplying disciples. Adding means I reach one person at a time and focus on doing that the rest of my life. That is a wonderful and God-honoring aspiration. Multiplying, however, means I not only reach people God leads me to, but I practice 3-D and train those I lead to reach others, who in turn reach others. Here's what it looks like on a chart. Let's use a cycle of 33 years, which corresponds to the years our Lord was on earth.

Witness-Life by Addition	Witness-Life by Multiplication
YEAR 1 (I lead 4 people to Jesus.) = **5**	**YEAR 1** (I lead 1 person to Jesus.) = **2**
YEAR 10 (I lead 5 more each year.) = **50**	**YEAR 10** (I continue leading 1 person a year to Jesus and those I led each lead 1 a year.) = **1,024**
YEAR 20 (I lead 5 more each year.) = **100**	**YEAR 20** (I and those led each lead 1.) = **1,048,576**
YEAR 30 (I lead 5 more each year.) = **150**	**YEAR 30** (I and those led each lead 1.) = **1,073,741,824**
YEAR 33 (I lead 5 more each year.) = **165**	**YEAR 33** (I and those led each lead 1.) = **8,589,934,592**

What an astounding contrast. By addition, my efforts might result in 165 people converted in 33 years. By multiplying and helping each one I reach to reach another, it results in more than 8.5 billion people rescued. It is through the multiplying of disciples that the whole world will hear

WE ARE CALLED BY GOD TO LIVE A WITNESS-LIFE AND TO TRAIN AND INSPIRE OTHERS TO DO THE SAME. WHAT A GREAT ASPIRATION.

the gospel and receive the opportunity to meet Jesus Christ. We are called by God to live a Witness-Life and to train and inspire others to do the same. What a great aspiration.

How do we prepare others to share their faith as a way of life? One way is to use the contents of this book to teach and inspire others to enter into the Witness-Life. Each chapter can be a lesson. Read a chapter or two per week, and talk about it with those you are training. Share examples from your own life. Remember those examples can and should be both successes and mistakes you've made and are making. Thus you would be imparting the truths of the Prayer, Care, Share life with them through the story of your own life. Make sure you have your disciple(s) work hard on their Journey with Jesus and Converting stories (Share 2) and on God's Story (Share 3). Practice with each other often.

May God's command to "be fruitful, and multiply" (Genesis 1:28 KJV) take on a new meaning for you. Let's multiply disciples who make disciples who make disciples.

> **3 Actions:** Prayer, Care, Share

> **2 Attitudes:** Dare and Hanging in There

> **1 Aspiration:** Prepare Others

> Here's how they all tie together:

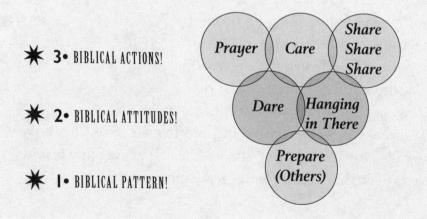

✳ **3•** BIBLICAL ACTIONS!

✳ **2•** BIBLICAL ATTITUDES!

✳ **1•** BIBLICAL PATTERN!

APPENDIX

Learning Gospel Apologetics:
Making a defense for the faith without getting defensive

WHEN our firstborn daughter, Tara, was young, she had a vivid and wonderful imagination. One night Marie and I watched a television special of *Peter Pan* with Tara and her younger sister, Courtney. They were, I think, about six and four years old. We were excited about watching this with them. After all, we thought, it was a famous children's story. But I didn't account for Tara's imagination. The scenes of the pirates and the Indians battling the children in Neverland were enough to send her imagination soaring.

As I put the girls in bed that night, Tara was very frightened. Somehow she thought she saw pirates and Indians as shadows on the wall in her room just above her bed. I told her that there were no scary pirates or Indians there but that it was her imagination at work. My rational explanation did little good. That's when her little sister spoke up. Fortunately the girls shared a room, so at least she had her younger sister near her as her imagination ran wild. Her sister said, "Tara, if you have Jesus in your heart, you don't have to be afraid." It was good theology from a four year old. We prayed together, and both girls made it through the night by faith and not by sight!

In the Witness-Life, most believers are afraid of the "big"

questions pre-Christians might ask. In our minds, we imagine situations where we will be asked one or more of these big questions and not know the answers, or at least not a full answer. These are the shadows on the wall. I will tackle four of the key questions seekers and skeptics ask and provide brief responses. I'll also give the titles of several resources that may be of help to go deeper on these matters.

One thing that might help readers is to realize and come to terms with the fact that for the big questions, we don't have full answers. This shouldn't surprise or alarm us. When finite humans try to comprehend the ways of an infinite God who created a complex universe, we never get the final word.

I recall the years I spent in seminary preparing to be a pastor and teacher. I was hopeful my studies in theology would bring satisfactory and final answers to the nature of God and human existence. In my systematic theology courses, brilliant professors expounded on great doctrines such as the nature of God, salvation, eternity, and more. At first it was exciting, then it was frustrating, and finally it led to worship. It was exciting because I was studying God with minds far greater than my own both in the classroom and the voluminous readings of other great minds on the great doctrines. It was like being on a gigantic treasure hunt with world-class guides. But then it got frustrating because at the end of every lecture and book, I was left with incomplete answers. There was simply no clear and complete understanding of any of the great themes. Mystery was everywhere. Finally, that mystery led to worship. I realized that though the study of every doctrine led to an incomplete ending, God kept getting larger and larger. Like Lucy in "The Chronicles of Narnia" series, who said that each time she saw Aslan he seemed larger, I saw that God and His ways were far beyond my limited brain capacity to understand them. This led to greater adoration of an almighty and transcendent God.

The questions we'll look at will, I hope, excite you, then frustrate you, then draw you to greater adoration of our Lord and God. You'll not only gain some plausible insights but also you may be drawn to a deeper worship of your Lord. Those are two wonderful benefits—wisdom and worship!

Two passages offer guidance as we enter the world of gospel apologetics. The first comes from the Apostle Paul and the second from Peter. Knowing of their experience traveling throughout the Roman Empire engaging with seekers and skeptics, they should be able to give us a lot of help.

> *Be wise in the way you act toward outsiders; make the most of every opportunity. Let your conversation be always full of grace, seasoned with salt, so that you may know how to answer everyone.*
>
> —Colossians 4:5–6

Always be prepared to give an answer to everyone who asks you to give the reason for the hope that you have. But do this with gentleness and respect, keeping a clear conscience, so that those who speak maliciously against your good behavior in Christ may be ashamed of their slander.

—1 Peter 3:15–16

I draw four areas of instruction from these passages. These principles prepare us to engage in gospel apologetics:

— PREPARATION —

We need to be prepared. We need wisdom that comes from God and that is received first by prayer. "If any of you lacks wisdom, you should ask God, who gives generously to all without finding fault, and it will be given you" (James 1:5). Pray for wisdom before you engage in an apologetic conversation, and pray during it! If you are like me, sometimes I hear a question or an assertion, and my mind doesn't know how to respond. At such times—and they are common—I turn to God in silent prayer before responding to the person I'm engaging. Ask for wisdom.

Secondly, study and learn how to give responses to these questions. Colossians says to be ready so that we "know" how to answer. We are to be wise in our words and wise in our actions. Paul told young Timothy to study to show himself approved (2 Timothy 2:15). Reading in the area of gospel apologetics and talking with other believers who are called to this ministry can help inform and prepare you. And remember, as I spoke about in the Dare chapter, it's OK—and in fact can be good—if you don't know an answer. It gives you opportunity to study the matter and have another appointment with the person who asked you the question.

— CONVERSATION —

Notice that the text speaks of such interactions as conversations, not lectures. That requires all the skills and patience, written about in Share I, regarding listening deeply and asking questions.

— ANSWER —

In both of the passages, we are encouraged to know how to answer questions and respond to assertions. This suggests that we don't have to initiate gospel apologetics but rather respond to apologetic issues when we are asked. I would rather spend my conversation time with a seeker, telling him or her about Jesus and what He has done for me and the world through His rescue mission than talk about the authority of Scripture, absolute truth, or evolution versus creation. Only go to gospel apologetics when your listener and inquirer seek to.

— MANNER OF CONVERSATION —

Our speech in gospel apologetics is to be full of grace (God's overwhelming love for the listener coming through us) and balanced with gentleness and respect. The character we display matters as much as—and sometimes more than—the content we deliver. Such conversations are not about whom is right or wrong. You can win an argument while losing a soul if you are out to win rather than to love.

A young pastor friend told me a story from his life. In a large family gathering, one member passionately argued how ridiculous it was to deny evolution. My friend decided to engage his family member by matching her passion and— in his words—"destroy her argument publicly" as more and more of the family gathered to watch the battle. As he told me this part of the story, he grew sad and said, "I know I will never be able to lead her to Christ." His need to win the argument trumped his words, and he didn't behave like Jesus at all. He's afraid he's lost the right to be heard in her life, and it grieves him.

We'll now take a look at four of the most common questions or assertions I've seen raised against Christianity by seekers and skeptics. I find these are most commonly asked when people are generally interested in learning more about Christianity.

There is much more to say on each of the four assertions. I have purposely kept my responses brief. I've mentioned several resources to help you go deeper should you desire. But please remember these issues are not presented so you can win an argument. I want you to join God in winning souls. Therefore please remember your character of gentleness, openness, and kindness matter as much as your content. Note also that the way I address each subject is to imagine I am actually talking with someone generally wanting to learn more and wants to be heard in their frustrations toward our faith. I present each of them keeping in mind the four principles from Scripture we just diagnosed.

THE BIBLE AS TRUSTWORTHY

ASSERTION: The Bible has been written and rewritten so many times it is really not accurate. It is full of mistakes. Why should I believe it is true?

RESPONSE: It sounds like you may have studied this issue somewhat. Tell me more about what you've learned.

LISTEN: To all they wish to say on the subject. Listen to God, and ask for wisdom in how to respond.

ENGAGE: (What follows are some possible responses.)

◆ Christians do believe that the Bible is trustworthy. We also believe it is more than philosophy and history. It is God's love letter to the world.

- ◆ The Bible tells us about God's love and His desire to have a personal relationship with all people.

- ◆ Even though the NIV Bible has more than 700,000 words, it has one central idea—restoration. It reveals God's long-range plan to make everything that is wrong in the world and us right and to restore the way it was created to be.

- ◆ Even though the Bible was written over a 1,600-year time period by more than 40 different authors from different walks of life on three different continents, it is consistent in its theme. It contains multiple genres of literature, including history, poetry, prophecy, letters, and logic, yet it is consistent in its description of God, people, suffering, hope, and God's rescue mission.

Pause and ask: Can I tell you a few things about the Bible that may help you trust its message and claims a bit more? (If the answer is yes, continue.)

- ◆ Some people say that the Bible is full of mistakes. However, we know that the Bible was copied by scribes who took their job very seriously. They had a system for copying with rigorous controls. They counted letters and words, and they had proofreaders. Still, some minor errors crept in. Yet none of the variances change the meaning of any passage. Out of all the words in the

New Testament, only 1 percent have significant variance from the earliest and most reliable texts. They are noted on the bottom of the page in my Bible. I am happy to show them to you.

◆ In 1947 a massive archaeological find in Israel revealed further proof of the Bible's accuracy. Scrolls of ancient documents were found in caves preserved in earthen jars. One jar held a scroll dated to BC 125. This scroll matched with more than 95 percent accuracy to the Hebrew Masoretic Text, from which our Old Testament was translated.

◆ In addition to historical accuracy, the amount of manuscripts relating to any passage or book in the Scriptures or any other work of history argue for the historical validity of the work. There are nearly 5,700 New Testament manuscripts and/or fragments of manuscripts in Greek (the language is which the New Testament was written) dating as early as the second century that exist. Many historical texts other than the Bible are considered trustworthy with only a few remaining manuscripts.

◆ Copies of New Testament manuscripts were written within decades of the historical events. Contrast that with other works of ancient literature. For instance, the earliest dated manuscript of Homer's *Iliad* is dated 500 years after the original. The earliest dated manuscript of Plato's *Tetralogies* was written 1,200 years after the original. Those that study the validity of ancient documents say that in general, the historical proximity of the document to the actual event is a key way to measure authenticity.

◆ There are approximately 20,000 handwritten copies of the New Testament in languages other than the original Greek language, which shows the importance the New Testament documents had to multiple cultures.

◆ Finally, the wisdom content of the Bible has been placed in multiple books throughout Western history. To remove the books with quotes or alluded content of the Bible in them from Western ideas would be to remove most of the books published! The Bible has greatly influenced Euro-American thought and literature for 2,000 years. Doesn't this suggest there is something to it?

If you'd like to know more about this issue, Josh McDowell's book, *Evidence that Demands a Verdict*, goes deeper into these issues. I also use a fine English Standard Version study Bible. As you can see, for me to use the Bible as authority is not just a leap of faith. It is based on solid accepted principles for judging historical validity. Most of all, it shows me how to know God personally. May I share with you, in just a couple of minutes, how that happened?

RELIGIOUS ARROGANCE

ASSERTION: Why does Christianity claim to be the only way to God? Isn't that ultimate arrogance?

RESPONSE: It seems you are questioning why Christianity—or perhaps any religion, for that matter—would claim exclusive truth and the only way to God. I'd like to hear more about why that is troubling to you.

LISTEN: To all they wish to say on the subject. Listen to God, and ask for wisdom in how to respond.

ENGAGE: Pluralism is popular in Western culture but not in every kind of endeavor. The notion of pluralism is that people are free to hold their view on an idea even if their view differs from others. When combined with relativism, pluralism means not only can I hold my contrary view but that my idea is equally true to yours. Yet, we don't agree that pluralism is acceptable when it comes to all moral issues. For instance, when an adult chooses to murder an innocent child, hardly anyone will accept they had the right to believe that was an appropriate belief and even worse, to act on it.

Similarly, in the world of mathematics, no one believes various pluralistic views on the nature of 2+2 are open to debate. To say it doesn't equal 4 is unacceptable. So pluralism is not always acceptable, and relativism even less so. Yet when it comes to religion, many argue for robust pluralism and relativism. Is this tenable?

Religious people don't believe all religions are equally true. Rick Mattson, in his book *Faith Is Like Skydiving*, makes the point that while all religions are about religion, they are not the same any more than a shelf of books in a bookstore say the same things because they are books. They are only the same in that they are bound, contain pages of words, and stack similarly. Once you open the books, their messages are very different.

◆ When pluralists argue that all religions are of equal value, they claim to know more about the religions than the believers in those religions, who don't believe all religions are equally true. Thus, they are violating their own argument for pluralism. Rather than valuing other people's views, they become, as Mattson puts it, know-it-alls disregarding others' views.

◆ Christians claim Christianity is the only way to God. The other world religions say the same to varying degrees. Therefore, to disregard Christianity because of its exclusive claim is to also disregard other religions for the same reason.

◆ Christianity claims to be exclusively true because its Founder, Jesus Christ, made the claim. Therefore, Christians would urge any religiously curious person to study the life of Jesus Christ and His claims and actions to determine whether His exclusive claim can possibly be true. He is the expert on Himself and

His diagnosis of God and humanity. Again, Christians aren't being arrogant when they say Christianity is the only way to God and eternal life, it is the Founder who made the claim. Christians merely report what the boss has said.

◆ The mid-twentieth-century Cambridge and Oxford professor C. S. Lewis laid out three alternatives for evaluating Jesus. In his book, *Mere Christianity*, he posits the now famous argument that has been summarized this way: Jesus was either a liar, a lunatic, or Lord. Since then, a fourth consideration has been posited that He is a legend made epic over time. Again, Christians would simply ask religiously curious people to take some time to study the internal and external evidence surrounding Jesus' life, death, and Resurrection before deciding in which of the categories He belongs.

◆ Christians will argue a twofold uniqueness of Christianity over other world religions. The first difference is the belief that good behavior qualifies one for the approval of God. Judaism, Islam, and Hinduism all in varying degrees argue that good behavior contributes to one's salvation or position with God or gods. Christianity says no one is good enough to please God but that God accepts those who place their trust in Him on the basis of Jesus' goodness and not their own. More, He takes the penalty for sin on Himself, resulting in complete and total forgiveness of all sins for all who trust in

Him. This is all God's doing and not mankind's.

◆ The second uniqueness is the doctrine of the Resurrection from the dead. An analogy of a religious founder or leader graveyard has often been used in this conversation. Mohammed's grave says *occupied*. Buddha's grave says *occupied*. Confucius's grave says occupied. Only the grave of Jesus says *empty*. Christians believe He is more than a historical religious leader; He lives today and forever in relationship with His people. Further, by conquering death He paved the way for believers to do the same and have everlasting life with Him. This is what Christians believe.

I personally discovered this in my late teens and early twenties. May I take a couple of minutes to tell you how knowing God personally happened for me?

SUFFERING AND INJUSTICE

ASSERTION: You speak about a living God of absolute power and absolute love, and yet we live in a world of suffering and horrible injustice. This makes no sense.

RESPONSE: Nothing makes me doubt my faith more than this issue. You are right that it's hard to make sense of it. On the surface it would seem that God is either not all-powerful or not all-loving or that there is no God. Before I try to make some sense of this from a Christian worldview, tell me, how does your worldview deal with this issue of unjust suffering and injustice?

LISTEN: To all they wish to say on the subject. Listen to God, and ask for wisdom in how to respond.

ENGAGE: Christian faith can be like sci-fi or fantasy in that a lot of its beliefs are not of this world. But one thing can be said for it—it doesn't shy away from any issue or problem. The God Story contained in the Bible offers an answer to the problem of suffering and injustice, but that answer is not complete and won't be until Christ returns as promised, when He will make right everything that is wrong in us and the world.

◆ When God created the world, He created it out of love, and it was good. There was no suffering or injustice. Humankind was the zenith of His creation. He made humans in His own image with the capacity to freely return His love.

◆ To freely return God's love meant that man had the choice to do so. Even in God's perfect Garden in the first chapters of the Bible, He placed a tree of the knowledge of good and evil and told man to not eat from it. Choice was a part of creation. In their freedom, man and woman disobeyed God, took the fruit from the tree, and thus possessed the knowledge not only of good but also evil. The knowledge of evil is what has led to evil behavior and the breaking of everything. We live in a broken and sad world because evil was set loose. Christianity believes evil is resident in varying degrees in all of us and all things.

◆ The world today contains both moral evil (freely chosen by humans) and natural evil (creation out of control). Examples of the first evil would be Hitler, a child-abuser, and the selfish bent in all humanity afflicting our thoughts and actions. Examples of natural evils are tsunamis and earthquakes. The lists of what contribute to each evil are nearly endless. People choose moral evil. People are faced with natural evil they did not cause. This is the Christian worldview—a perfect world now broken.

◆ Why doesn't an all-powerful and all-loving God stop it now? The Christian answer is complex and incomplete. We believe He can—because He has authority over all things in heaven and earth (Matthew 28:18; Colossians 1:15) and that He works out everything in conformity with the purpose of His will (Ephesians 1:11). We believe He is slowly and gradually working to restore humanity and the world to Himself. For more on this see Mattson's book *Faith Is Like Skydiving* as mentioned in the question on religious pluralism.

◆ Why so slow? The best I can offer on the slowness is to consider the alternative. If God stopped all evil now, it would require the destruction of all humanity since sin or moral evil is our choice. To eradicate it would be to eradicate us, and that's not a pleasant solution. Secondly, He has human beings throughout the world that He wants to know Him and be rescued from their sin, not destroyed by it. So, He is restoring slowly and gradually through the extension of His kingdom and the gift of His Son, Jesus, who died to forgive our moral evil. Finally, the biblical evidence is voluminous—a day is coming when slow and gradual is done. He will bring judgment against all sin and injustice and a new heaven and perfect earth for those who love Him and made Him Lord of their lives.

◆ While we live in the world of suffering and injustice, He promises to be with us (Matthew 28:20) and to provide His grace to sustain us in all ways necessary. Sometimes He intervenes with miraculous healing and justice. Other times He permits evil to flourish but never without His presence and protection. Neither temptation nor crisis shall break us (1 Corinthians 10:13; 2 Corinthians 4:8–9).

◆ Jesus suffered too. God the Son knows our sorrows and has experienced our injustices. He was born into the world of winter cold and virulent disease. He was a refugee infant fleeing with His parents from a tyrannical leader seeking His life. As a man, He suffered rejection from His family, disloyalty from His friends, and unfair treatment from the government and the religious institution. He was physically abused, beaten, and crucified.

He knew He was born to suffer and be mistreated (John 12:27). He knows our sorrows, our endless frustration, and our longing for wrong to be right. He lived it.

◆ So, Christianity is about a God who will end all wrong, who is with us until that occurs, and has felt all we feel. Even our longing for right and our hatred of our wrong is a sign it will not always be this way.

I was suffering deeply when I came to experience God personally. May I take just a couple of minutes to tell you how that happened?

SEXUAL MORALITY

ASSERTION: You Christians are mean. You tell people how they are to behave sexually. Further, your ethic disallows the value of two loving people committing to each other in marriage outside of a male-female relationship. You say your God is love. If so, why aren't you?

RESPONSE: I understand that my worldview does conflict with that of many people in our country and the Western world. I'd like to respond to that but before I do, may I ask you a follow-up question? Have your views of sexuality and marriage always been what they are, or have they evolved? If they have evolved, what led you to the position you hold now?

LISTEN: To all they wish to say on the subject. Listen to God, and ask for wisdom in how to respond.

ENGAGE:

◆ God created sexuality and marriage. Both were practiced in the perfect world He created at the beginning of human existence (Genesis 1–2). They were part of what God called "very good." When humans chose to disobey God by acquiring the knowledge of evil and choosing to run their lives apart from Him, all manner of disorder and dysfunction spread on the earth. Christianity speaks of two kinds of evil that were loosed by that early choice. The first is moral evil (free choices made by humans) and natural evil (nature itself set loose).

◆ God, in His wisdom, created sex and marriage in such a way as to provide the greatest good to His Creation. If you will, He put a fence of protection around both the practices to keep them pure and right. Within the fence they enable people to flourish. Climb over or break through the fence, and all manner of disorder and disintegration ensues. Hugh Hefner, the founder of the pornographic magazine *Playboy*, once said, "The major civilizing force in the world is not religion; it is sex." That is the ultimate statement of climbing over the fence. Sex was intended to be a good part of life, but not the civilizing force. The Bible says that any time humans take something good and elevate it to a god, it is idolatry. Such is the case with sex outside the fence. We believe that only God and a relationship with Him can be the true and perfect civilizing force in lives and nations. So let's look at a few of God's fences.

Fence 1: Sex is designed to be a flourishing activity within the confines of marriage and only marriage. We believe that sex is far more than just a physical event. It is a spiritual, psychological, and physical reality (1 Corinthians 6:13–18). Only the lifelong commitment of marriage is strong enough to sustain all three aspects of sex. It is the "superglue." This is why we urge people to not be involved in sexual practices outside of marriage. Sex is a powerful part of the life force. It's kind of like fire and heat. They offer warmth and cleansing power. But unbridled, they destroy.

Fence 2: Pornography is a fantasizing of sexuality in ways that cannot be met by real life. Pornography destroys the act of sexuality as the ultimate act of giving and repackages it as one of taking. It is addictive and can psychologically enslave those who engage with it. It destroys marital fidelity and distorts the sexual expectations of singles and married couples. This is why Jesus was so adamant in warning people to not even look upon another to lust for them (Matthew 5:27–30).

Fence 3: Sexuality and marriage are created for one man and one woman. I realize there is a growing societal bent toward affirming same-gender sexuality and marriage, but God's sacred writings make it clear it was designed for male and female (Genesis 2). Our physical makeup even supports this. This doesn't mean that some people don't have same-sex attraction or opposite-sex orientation. Attraction and orientation are not sinful. But the acting out of those desires is where the fence comes down.

Glenn Stanton has written extensively on this issue in his fine book, *Loving My (LGBT) Neighbor.* He refers to respected research that indicates approximately 4–6 percent of the US population have same-sex attraction. So, does the Christian worldview deny the right for homosexual persons to have sexual relationships? No. Christianity has no right to deny it. Christianity is a spiritual worldview not a governmental control agency. But it has the responsibility to say that homosexual practice is breaking through a fence that God intended to protect people not to enslave them. We would affirm our position not because we are mean-spirited but, rather, because our warnings are acts of love. When my little boy was about to walk into a street of passing cars, I yelled as loudly as possible to stop. I am so glad he stopped before he was hurt. This is how we think regarding sexuality outside of the fence.

You may say if homosexual attraction is outside of God's will, then why did He make some people this way? The verdict is still out as to whether homosexual attraction is biological or environmental or a combination of both factors. But even if it is biological, or the way people are made, Christianity would argue that natural evil is a reality in this world. There are tsunamis and tornadoes and people with mental and physical disabilities from birth. Homosexual attraction is a part of the reality of a fallen human nature. It is not the way God created it to be, but it is the way things are in a broken world. All evils and sorrows will one day disappear, but we live in a broken world until then.

Fence 4: Sexuality and marriage are not merely physical. There is a deep longing in all people for intimacy and sexuality. Marriage provides a way to fill part of that need. God provides meaningful friendships for companionship and nonsexual intimacy. All persons can enjoy the great gift of intimate friendships. Yet, all human relationships fall short and leave us longing. No marriage, sexual expression, or human friendship will fill the longing for intimacy completely, though they are wonderful as far as they go. God intended fulfillment only in relationship with Him.

I believe that only in your relationship with God will you find true, satisfying intimacy. In fact when one has discovered intimacy with God, the other intimacies grow stronger as well. May I tell how I have begun to experience this in my life?

A Prayer, Care, Share Devotional Guide

by Marie Allison

NOTHING helps a Christian in the Witness-Life as much as deepening our love for God through regular interaction with Him. Prayer, Bible reading, and reflection are dynamic life-enhancing means for intimacy with God. Following are some ways to enter into these practices. Lon and I have designed these to help you for 20 minutes a day, five days a week, for five weeks. Of course, you can use them in other patterns, and repeating them can also be a blessing. Enjoy your life with God and your life in witness!

Before you begin: Prepare your heart by praying, *Lord, cleanse my heart so You can speak to me through the Scriptures. Make my mind alert, my soul active, and my heart responsive. Surround me with Your presence during this time.*

◆ **10 Minutes:** Listen to God (Scripture Reading)

◆ **5 Minutes:** Journal

◆ **5 Minutes:** Talk to God (Prayer)

— YOU WERE MADE FOR THIS! —

PASSAGE	✓	DATE
Matthew 28:16–20	❏	_____
2 Corinthians 5:11–21	❏	_____
1 Corinthians 3:1–15	❏	_____
John 4:1–26	❏	_____
John 4:27–38	❏	_____

• • • • • •

Reflection	❏	_____
Reflection	❏	_____